Understanding
the Recovering
Alcoholic

KENNETH ANONYM

Second Edition, published by Hazelden Foundation
July, 1980. All rights reserved.

Library of Congress Catalog Card Number: 73-20859

Copyright 1974 by

ALBA HOUSE COMMUNICATIONS
Canfield, Ohio 44406

ISBN: 0-89486-103-4

Dedication

To all of us who have come to
understand the realistic meaning
of being
alcoholic in recovery.

Acknowledgements

I wish to express my gratitude to Dr. Don Cahalan, Professor of Behavioral Science, School of Public Health, University of California; Dr. Max Weisman, Director of the Division of Alcoholism Control, State Dept. of Mental Hygiene, Baltimore, Maryland; and Mrs. Marty Mann, President of the National Council on Alcoholism, for their reading of the manuscript and very helpful suggestions.

I am also grateful to Mr. Edward Cone of the Alcoholics Anonymous Information Center, Castro Valley, California, for his time and effort in typing out this manuscript.

Contents

Preface

One hundred million Americans drink and ten million are estimated to be alcoholics. These facts speak for themselves in the need for understanding the recovery of alcoholics. The vast majority of our alcoholics go untreated either out of ignorance of the disease or out of sheer neglect, a neglect by alcoholics themselves in the belief that they are not alcoholic and also by significant others ashamed of the social taboo of alcoholism.

Understanding the Recovering Alcoholic is not another "here's how" book theorizing on the puzzling game of getting off the sauce. At the present time, experts disagree on the causes and "cure" of alcoholism, and the vast majority of the alcoholic population couldn't care less. This book is addressed to the alcoholic who is scared enough to care enough to give recovery a try; because he or she has had it with being tired of a drug misuse that is nothing short of gradual suicide. Alcohol is a drug, and alcoholics' misuse of it comprises the largest segment of America's drug scene.

Alcohol is a neutral spirit. For most people who imbibe, it is a recreational drug served in a variety of beverages. In our social rituals, alcohol drinking has an honored place, yet, like every drug, there are dangers of side effects and habituation. Alcoholics are living casualties of the misuse of this chemical. They have somehow passed the thin line of normal drinking. Their drinking is pathological. These people need treatment far more than moralizing judgment.

The focus of this book is on understanding — the self-understanding which is the mainspring of vital personal recovery of the alcoholic. There are medical techniques available, but the alcoholic must want to make them work. The chronic, recurrent disease of alcoholism demands an on-going life-style of total sobriety to arrest it. You see, there is no magic pill! This is a question of control, self-control; but where and how does the alcoholic achieve this control? What better place than in a fellowship of alcoholics who are achieving recovery?

There are many thousands of these people in our communities throughout the nation in the fellowship of Alcoholics Anonymous (AA).

Understanding the Recovering Alcoholic is an interpersonal reflection on attitudes and action basic to recovery experienced in AA groups. It is the story of an alcoholic in recovery told from inside alcoholism, addressed to fellow alcoholics and to significant others related to them — family, friends, employers, doctors and clergy — who are in need of understanding what recovery means as a way of life, and it is only in life that recovery takes place. No one can write out a sure-cure prescription. There is no one formula that governs it. It must come to the alcoholic in the art of his or her living. Perhaps in our "enlightened age," we are hearing too much about the science of recovery and not enough about the art of doing it in recovering the sober self.

When one considers the epidemic proportions of alcoholism in America today, there is a general need in our society for this understanding toward recovery in our most untreated treatable disease. There is special need for understanding that goes beyond a strictly medical model of recovery, to recovery in personal living.

Dr. Andrew Malcolm in his excellent work, *The Pursuit of Intoxication,* wrote:

> In treating alcoholism, it is important to recognize the multifactorial nature of its etiology. Of course, it is a medical condition. Who can deny that cirrhosis and peptic ulcer and Wernicke's encephalepathy are medical disorders? But alcoholism is also a psychiatric illness, and it is a condition that interests anthropologists and sociologists and law enforcement agencies — indeed, practically everybody but shoemakers (unless the shoemaker happens also to be an alcoholic). Thus, I submit that it is now necessary for us to discard the strictly medical model into which we have attempted to press alcoholism since the passing of the moralistic and punitive period.

Dr. Malcolm, a psychiatrist with the Addiction Research Foundation in Toronto, pays high tribute to the work of AA in the alcoholic's recovery. "Of all the socially oriented programs, Alcoholics Anonymous is certainly the most effective. The contribution of this organization has been immense."

Let us examine in the following chapters the humanness of the alcoholic's disease and the interpersonal recovery life-style of the AA program. The story is human, all too human.

I. HUMAN, ALL TOO HUMAN

"Here was the first authentic clue after many years of fruitless effort." Dr. Harry M. Tiebout, Medical Panel, 20th Alcoholics Anonymous Convention.

Understanding the Recovering Alcoholic was begun in Michigan during the heavy snows of mid-winter. It sums up a personal understanding of Alcoholics Anonymous (AA) and the nation's number one health problem — alcoholism. There was ample time in many snowed-in days to reflect on what had taken place in my journey from the wet hell of a drinking alcoholic to the meaningful life of sobriety, and what I have encountered in the lives of many other recovering alcoholics in the moral miracle of AA.

This book is not about alcohol, but, precisely, alcoholism. It is not about people who drink or about people who occasionally overdrink. It concerns people who have lost control of their drinking. This is not an anti-drink book. It is an antidotal story for alcoholics.

My motive in writing is an invitation of hope for alcoholics in search of a way of motivating and maintaining a life-style of sobriety, an act of gratitude to my fellow alcoholics anonymous, and an attempt to inform the general public of the much misunderstood process of the alcoholic's disease.

Thoroughly aware of the preachy and moralizing rhetoric that has so sadly characterized writings on alcoholism in the Prohibition era, and which still endures in much of our American mores, the accent of this book is heavily on understanding people afflicted with an insidious disease, rather than moralizing judgment on self-inflicted bums. In a positive context, this book aims at telling about the alcoholic in recovery, and the help available in communities for those in need.

From the start, we should exorcize the demon-image of the alcoholic as the grave sinner penalized by divine wrath and come to understand the sickness that needs to be arrested in a human life. We are talking about a human, all-too-human illness. Understanding the alcoholic is, of course, a multifaceted endeavor, because alcoholics are prone to deny their illness using an infinite variety of games alcoholics play in order to dodge their real identities. "Recovery," in too many cases, is no more than bodily repairment so they can drink again and, thus, recycle themselves back to the emergency room of the local hospital.

Understanding drinking alcoholics in a spirit of hope for recovery is a hard task for the sober majority. In fact, we might call it a case of Mission Impossible, if it were not for the many thousands of recovering alcoholics in communities across the nation. We are endeavoring to understand an insidious disease that strikes at the total person, body and spirit, individually and socially. The story is perhaps best told from inside alcoholism, by alcoholics who have experienced its nightmare and the day by day route to recovery.

Does the term "drinking alcoholic" appear overly expressed, redundant to you? Perhaps you are given to the notion that all alcoholics drink, that is why they are alcoholics. If you are an alcoholic confirmed in a drinking career, or if you intimately or even casually know him or her, you may find the adjective "drinking" superfluously attached to "alcoholic." Of course the alcoholic drinks — what else? *Understanding the recovering alcoholic,* however, in terms of medical knowledge and AA experiences gives evidence that persons afflicted with the disease of alcoholism not only can stop drinking, but also many actually do stop and live without need for a drink. Yet the recovering are still alcoholics, because the disease is arrested but never cured. In this context we can justify the term "drinking alcoholics," since one can become a non-drinking alcoholic, which is what the recovering alcoholic is experiencing perhaps for the first time.

The theme of this book deals with a special kind of alcoholic, the recovering alcoholic. This is the man or woman already awakened to the basic admission and honest acceptance that "I am an alcoholic. I need help." It is our endeavor to explore the route of recovery as a life-style, a process of learning new goals, attitudes, and habits practiced by the vast majority of recovering alcoholics in some 16,000 groups across the nation.

Unfortunately, the larger segment of our alcoholic population is not in recovery. These people are in all walks of life, learned and unlearned, affluent, middle class, poor. They opt to continue their drinking careers, which are, in fact, a tragedy of gradual suicide. Perhaps this saga of AA recovery will serve some purpose toward their real self-understanding. It is my belief that every drinking alcoholic wants recovery in some way. It's the damned effort needed that kills their try.

Every recovering alcoholic in AA knows the vital value of total sobriety and what a mental, emotional, and physical battle he or she had to undergo to arrive at that admission and acceptance. "Total sobriety" is an alien phrase in the alcoholic's vocabulary during a drinking career. It means the impossible, a life empty, dried out of the stream of life, repressed, and frustrated. In sharp contrast, the dawning of recovery is in the personal inward discovery of a new and vital meaningfulness of sobriety and freedom from the slavery of alcohol addiction, in the hope of regaining human dignity. Just as sobriety has a uniquely negative meaning for the drinking alcoholic, so it takes on a uniquely positive meaning for the recovering alcoholic. It is our task in these reflections to portray sobriety as a life-style-for-life. It is more than a negative route of dry abstinence, an aversion for alcohol.

Most recovering alcoholics are men and women very much active in our communities. From all appearances, they are part of the scene of everyday life. The recovering alcoholic could be from any walk of life: a professional, a doctor, lawyer, or clergyman; a television actor, a worker on the assembly line, the postman who brings your morning mail, the housewife who lives next door. Our steps in recovery are taken in the everyday flow of life.

At one time or another the alcoholic in a hospital or sanatorium can understand that the rest test of recovery comes in everyday living, living one's life in the world. Institutional care is only the starting point of recovery. Meaningful recovery is an ongoing process, because the recurrence of the disease is only a drink away. How often we alcoholics experimented with this truth only to learn its bitter consequences. Recovery is a life-style-for-life. Recovery is more intensive and extensive than mere bodily recovery, to become physically fit again. The heart of the matter is, recovering the human spirit to live, to celebrate life, means the alcoholic cannot ingest alcoholic beverages and positively be involved in a life worth living.

Those Popular Alcoholic Myths

How curious is the popular myth that recovery is a hospital event, a pill-taking, restful sojourn, while others "recover" us? How many of us alcoholics have tried all that and failed to recover, because we never made an honest try for the spirit of sobriety in our lives? We mistook a legitimate part of recovery for the total recovery. We were getting well to drink again, moderately, of course. Maybe we were convinced that we could become social drinkers because we had learned a tragic lesson. And so we had to learn anew that drinking for us sooner or later means getting drunk. Alcoholism is an insidious disease of subtle symptoms that for too many of us does not begin to surface until it begins to destroy our lives. Symptoms, which unlike the symptoms of other diseases, the alcoholic tries artfully to conceal, and which he or she so often only unwillingly admits when brutally victimized.

Still, many alcoholics and their loved ones fight what they regard as the social stigma, the doomsday label "alcoholic." They are more concerned with what people say about the alcoholic than real treatment for recovery. In time, some come to understand that recovery for a person afflicted with the disease of alcoholism involves more than drying out a drunk; that the name of the game is not the number of drinks consumed, but the very act of drinking. Alcoholism infects the whole person in body, mind, and spirit. Recovery must influence the alcoholic's total life to arrest this disease, for which there is yet no cure.

Undoubtedly, one of the greatest myths on the American scene springs from our Puritan ethic, our drive to moralize every life situation, which enshrines the blessings of sobriety in successful people and entombs the alcoholics in the limbo of Skid Row. We are easily given to the belief that the alcoholic is a weak-willed person who "abuses" his or her life by excessive alcohol consumption. In the early decades of this century, we tried to correct this "abuse" by legislating prohibition and eliminating "the cause." Although the experiment failed, we still too often continue to moralize about alcoholism as if it were only a case of self-willed bad morals. Notwithstanding our age enlightened to alcoholism as a disease, we still prefer to speak about "alcohol abuse" or "intemperate drinkers" when it would be pointedly realistic to speak about the disease of alcoholism and drug addicts.

Recovering alcoholics are particular targets for uninformed and misinformed understanding because they are in a sort of twilight zone as alcoholics and are recovering. Some people are prone to moralize about them too heavily as drinking alcoholics. On the other hand, others are prone to moralize about them too heavily as recovered or "cured." This latter state of mind is commonly experienced by recovering alcoholics, whose friends cannot understand why he or she is not drinking socially now that "all is well" and one is "cured." Totally dry recovery looks to them like a case of moral scrupulosity, playing the field too carefully.

Our misunderstandings of recovery are more or less rooted in our misunderstanding of the definition of an alcoholic. The word has a wide spectrum of meanings, and the more we come to understand the private meanings given to it, the less we believe in an actual common usage. Still, we are easily given to the myth that because we all use the same word "alcoholic," we know exactly what it means. However, if we really bother to listen to one another, it should be plainly evident that our supposed common-understanding falls apart.

The word "alcoholic" covers a forest of meanings shaped by religious, ethnic, social class, and geographical factors. More important than the intellectual understanding of the word is the emotional impact that it bears, especially when it is applied to oneself or a significant other. In more common usage in America, "alcoholic" does not carry primarily a medical significance of an illness so much as it still bears heavily pejorative moralizing tones. For many it is a doomsday label. More commonly, people try to avoid the word "alcoholic" as an identity tag. Although the term varies in the seriousness and social taboo that it bears (from the strict censures of the traditional Jewish and Oriental families to the more tolerant drinking attitudes of peoples from Northern Europe), there is a commonly basic image that the alcoholic is a drunkard. When this person recovers to a sober life-style, it is erroneously believed that he or she is no longer alcoholic. We are talking about alcohol addicts and not just spoiled social drinkers who recover from a bad drinking night on the town.

The AA fellowship has contributed in a large measure toward dispelling this myth, but it still endures in the minds of many with sad consequences for the addict who tries drinking after his or her hospital "recovery." The AA experience, since its beginning in the thirties, has advocated the life-long endurance of the alcoholic disease in the addicted. AA admits that alcoholism is a complex disease involving spiritual, mental, and bodily disorders, and that the alcoholic can recover spiritually, mentally, and bodily, but not from his or her loss of control in drinking. It is basic to recovery therapy that the alcoholic stops drinking.

AA's insistence on abstinence leads some people to believe that AA is no more than a stop-drinking program. People who should know better are too often found mouthing this criticism. For the most part, the AA recovery life-style aims at building the human back into the alcoholic's life by a character transformation of the whole person. Alcohol is only mentioned once in the Twelve Steps of the AA program. There can be no doubt, however, that AA strives throughout its program to impress upon its members the vital importance of not taking that first drink. The fellowship is for alcoholics and not just any neurotic, or sick-livered person, or whatever.

Alcoholic drinking is at the core of what sets off the disease in the addicted. Resentments, impatience, particular repressions, and frustrations are dynamic forces within the alcoholic that bring about alcoholic drinking in a constitution disposed to this disease. Recovery involves the total person, moral and physical. AA endeavors to counsel the alcoholic to seek medical and/or psychological aid, when such need is present. The fellowship does not claim to be a substitute for these disciplines. AA aims at motivating and maintaining a life-style sobriety in alcoholics who want its help.

Problem Drinkers and a Number One Health Problem, U.S.A.

Doctor Roger Egeberg, while he was Assistant Secretary for Health and Scientific Affairs, Department of Health, Education, and Welfare, declared alcoholism, among other effects on our national health, a number one health problem in America. Although the disease is treatable, it remains untreated in a large portion of our alcoholic population, which the National Institute on Alcohol Abuse and Alcoholism estimates at some 10 million alcoholics. The number is undoubtedly larger. One of ten drinkers in the nation is alcoholic. Personal and public harm due to overindulgence is escalating to skyrocketing proportions. It would be false to assume, of course, that everyone who harms himself and/or others by overindulgence has the disease of alcoholism. There is more to the diagnosis. However, we can opine that the larger percentage are alcoholics already afflicted by the disease and that a large number are candidates for the disease. The illness is among the five leading diseases killing Americans. Some 100 million Americans over the age 15 are consumers of alcohol.

There is no typical person suffering from alcoholism. Less than three percent of alcoholics are found on Skid Row. Among men, drinking problems occur most frequently in their early twenties and among women most frequently in their thirties and forties. Since World War II, the number of known women alcoholics has doubled.

The human loss to individuals, families, and communities is difficult to calculate. Between six and ten percent of employees have a drinking problem. The total cost to the nation is nearly $43 billion a year due to absenteeism, health and welfare services, and property damages. Lost production alone due to alcoholism has been estimated at $19.64 billion annually.

Among drinking teenagers, 3.3 million are showing signs that may lead to the development of alcoholism. In the last several years, researchers have conducted a number of studies on infants born to women who drank heavily during pregnancy. A significant number of these infants are born with a definite pattern of physical, mental, and behavioral abnormalities which researchers have named the "Fetal Alcohol Syndrome."

Fifty percent of all fatal car accidents involve alcohol. Among violent crimes, 65% of the murders, 40% of the assaults, 55% of the fights or assaults in the home, and 60% of child abuse cases are alcohol related. These *Facts on Alcoholism*, published by the National Institute on Alcohol Abuse and Alcoholism, highlight the current catastrophic features of this epidemic.

Alcoholism is treatable. The situation is not hopeless. Leading clinical therapists report recovery rates of 50 to 70%. Effective business and industry employee alcoholism programs indicate recovery rates of 65 to 80%. Alcoholics Anonymous in its world-wide fellowship has an estimated membership in excess of one million, of which 356,383 are in North America. This program for motivating and maintaining recovery is most commonly utilized for this disease which, although it cannot be cured, can be brought under control by total abstinence in normal productive living. Approximately 80% of AA members who stay sober between one and five years will remain in the fellowship.

Problem drinking for the person who drinks out of the disease of alcoholism does not simply pass away in time so that he or she can drink normally. The bottom line is that drinking is the problem of the alcohol addict for life. Recovery that is realistic must focus on total abstinence in a life worth living.

In our American know-how, speed culture, some are easily given to the belief that an alcoholic's recovery can be packaged and delivered on order. How often we misunderstand the time dimension of recovery. We seize quick remedies such as brief, intensive, motivational therapy. Maybe we hope to shock the alcoholic out of his or her illness by sudden exposure to its frightening gravity.

The Federal Safety Act is currently providing such mini-programs for the drunken driver. It may work for the problem drinker, who does not have total loss of control, but for the alcoholic, we can bet on its failure. Alcoholism cannot disappear without sufficient and skillful therapy. What is needed is a program productive of a life-style to arrest the disease.

The Need for Understanding

In our wet culture, and it is getting wetter, there is a special need for human understanding of the recovery of the alcoholic as a person afflicted with an illness. There are some 155 synonyms in our language for intoxication that range from the prosaic words inebriation or drunkenness, to the more colorful slang of high or being stoned, and so forth. The recovering alcoholic knows only too well that all our words fail to describe the illness for what it is in its vital complexity.

Many books have been written about understanding the alcoholic. It is time that we accentuate the positive in attempting to understand what alcoholic recovery means for the person in his or her inward struggle to re-form a human life, to be restored to sanity of mind and health of body, to return soberly to family, livelihood, and position in society. There is more than an external rehabilitation involved here. There is an *inward character change* of a spiritual nature taking place in the recovering alcoholic person, and this is important for those around the recovering alcoholic to understand.

The kind of understanding we are talking about is more than matter-of-fact knowledge about alcoholism. It is, in essence, interpersonal understanding of fellow humans afflicted with a disease. For some of us, this means personal concern and commitment in helping our loved ones: a spouse, a son, a daughter, a relative, a friend. It could be a professional in the field of alcoholism aware of a patient as a fellow human. It could be an employer's sense of care for an employee in recovery. It may be understanding help for ourselves.

Unfortunately, too many of the sober majority are given in their sensitiveness to easy judgments of doubt and denial that an alcoholic is really recovering. "I would not employ that man. He has admitted that he has a drinking problem. Of course, he is trying to do something about it, but he is a bad risk by just being an alcoholic." "Do you really believe we should invite the Smiths to our home? Do you remember how he acted after a couple of drinks at that party several months ago? They say he is doing well in recovery, but you never know about alcoholics." "Better that the children stay away from that family across the street. I hear that she is an admitted alcoholic because she goes to AA meetings."

Do we really believe that an alcoholic can recover? What is really real about him or her? In self-understanding, we recovering alcoholics must admit that our past performances have not always been grounds for a reputation of trust and respect. The expertise of AA people is in the practical realm of showing "once an alcoholic always an alcoholic" need not mean a drinking alcoholic. The fact that so many thousands of AA people are recovering and recovered from the illness attests to this.

There is a personal and institutional understanding of the recovering alcoholic. Our personal understanding is most basic in the hope that enlightened persons will continue to effect understanding on institutional levels in government, industry, hospitals, churches, and other agencies that can aid the alcoholic in recovery. We must have personal openness and care for our fellow humans in need and not just rely on the cold facts of legislation, company policies, or church directives for understanding. Unless the awakening takes place in our personal lives, there will be no meaningful understanding of what recovery really is.

The understanding related in these chapters is from a personal inside view of alcoholism and what recovery entails. Understanding must begin inside us as people. Out of this personal consciousness of alcoholism as an illness and the process of recovery, comes social consciousness of the need for more research, more public education, more federal and state legislation that takes account of the disease concept of alcoholism. There is a need for more personnel policies in business and industry and the professions, more hospital facilities for our number one health problem.

The decision of the District of Columbia to obtain social and medical help for the homeless alcoholic rather than a jail sentence; the Hughes Bill, enacted as P.L. 91-616, mandating the Federal government to aid in recovery rather than discriminate against government employees sick with alcoholism, are progressive legal steps taken out of human understanding. The churches are also undergoing more humane understanding of this illness in reaction to pious condemnations of a self-inflicted vice. Many churches, formerly prohibitionist and moralistic toward alcoholics, are realizing that alcoholics are fellow humans in need of understanding and treatment.

Adequate funding of progressive legislation now on the books for the rehabilitation of the alcoholic is still wanting in practice in many communitites. There are too many instances where high-sounding policies are lost in a bureaucratic maze, where funds stated for alcoholic care are channelled to other

20

needs favored by the authorities. Why waste the money on revolving-door-drunks who are sobered up and are soon back again? Alcoholism, in too many instances, is the disease where the patient is blamed if the therapy fails.

Federal, state, and local governments are funding a significant proportion of the resources for alcoholism treatment. Still, alcoholism is the most neglected health problem in the United States today. It ranks second to heart disease in estimated number of total cases. In terms of support per victim, it is currently second to last in private support revenue. Muscular dystrophy, affecting 200,000 victims, ranks first.

Total dollar costs in alcoholism to the American economy are way above the liquor industry's tax payments. For states and municipalities, the cost-alcohol tax differential may be larger. The consumer movement has propelled us into an era of fair labeling practices and truth in advertising. There is good reason to legislate a warning label for alcoholic beverages similar to the one used for cigarettes. *This product could be hazardous to your health.*

Between 1971 and 1975, national survey responses showed an increasing awareness that alcohol is a drug and that it can be a fatal one. More respondents believed that drunkenness is: similar to an overdose of drugs, is an indication of alcoholism, and is a sign of social irresponsibility. Impressive changes were also found for several attitudes toward alcoholism — from 50 percent in 1971 to 37 percent in 1975 agreeing that there is no recovery from alcoholism.

This book is not meant to make a difficult topic simple. It does not call for any magic bullet to shoot down our popular alcoholic myths. Hopefully, it will contribute some understanding of recovery as a life-style to people who want to get well, available in the local AA group. This is not a medical or psychological work of professional expertise on the alcoholic disease. It is about an interpersonal appeal for understanding what happens to alcoholics during recovery and about the most successful attempts to motivate and maintain sobriety in day-by-day living — Alcoholics Anonymous. Our story is human, all too human. Really, it is not hard to understand on the human level. Alcoholics are not so different when we view them with even a tiny bit of wisdom. In recovery, they share in the common sorrows of a sick world and in the hope of a better world.

II. ALCOHOLISM, A DISEASE

The emotional impact of the statement, "Alcoholism is a sickness," is such that very few people care to stop to think what it actually means." — Dr. L.E. Wexberg, Quarterly Journal of Studies of Alcohol.

Would you believe that we alcoholics do our own kind of private moralizing about our drinking problems to escape the admission that we have the alcoholic disease? We carefully check our dissimilarities with the stories of admitted alcoholics. We do our best not to identify with them, and try to moralize our malaise as the result of a weak-willed response to some bad situation. Always the focus of the blame is lodged outside of ourselves. Perhaps we are given to believe that somehow the world is wrong, and we are victims of its social sins. When we cannot escape self-blame, we attempt to shift it to our past, as if now we have learned our lesson and we will control our drinking. All of this must be understood as part of the unfolding tragic drama of alcoholism. It is part of the activated total disease that the afflicted person fights his or her own identity.

It is becoming more and more difficult for alcoholics to hide their identity as victims of a disease. In past ages, they were more or less known to be sick, which is what intoxication means. In the Book of Proverbs we read:

Who has contentions? Who has ravings? Who has wounds without cause? Who has redness of eyes? They that tarry long at the wine; they that go to try mixed wine . . . At the last it bites like a serpent, and stings like a basilisk. Your eyes shall behold strange things, and your heart shall utter confused things . . . They have struck me, and I felt it not. They have beaten me, and I know it not. When shall I awake. I will seek it yet again. (Proverbs 23:25, 30, 32, 33, 35.)

This proverbial picture of the drunkard is certainly not the picture of a person healthy in spirit and body. Still, the medical diagnosis of alcoholism *as a disease* did not receive acceptance

23

until recently, and even now there are many who prefer to moralize it as a vice of evil-willed people. How very striking is the final verse of *Proverbs* describing the alcoholic illness. "When shall I awake? I will seek it yet again." *This is indeed the characteristic signal of the disease — the loss of control in drinking.*

The American Medical Association officially accepts alcoholism as a disease. Public health agencies, the National Council on Alcoholism and its local affiliates, and the fellowship of Alcoholics Anonymous contribute greatly in educating the public to the disease concept of alcoholism. Research in the relatively new field of alcohol studies reveals that what the physician in the past regarded as the disorder of alcoholism was in fact its end-result, complicated by the long effects, both physical and mental, of heavy consumption of alcohol over the years.

Medical coverage is becoming increasingly available through health protection sources. By 1976, only 4 out of 60 health plans responding to a survey excluded alcoholism treatment. Increasingly, comprehensive alcoholism benefits are being offered by Blue Cross plans. Twenty states have enacted legislation either mandating that alcoholism coverage be provided or requiring that it be available as an option. In ten states, alcoholism treatment is specifically provided for under social services for individual and families program (Title XX of the Social Security Act).

Occupational programs as a mechanism for early identification and intervention of alcoholic employees are receiving ever-increasing acceptance. By mid-1977, the number of organizations with some type of program had increased to nearly 2,400. This is a far brighter picture for recovery when one considers that, traditionally, the alcoholic employee was usually fired. When one considers that one out of every twenty employees has a drinking problem, it is incredible that many companies ignore treatment programs even though the disease concept of alcoholism has been scientifically established.

Our advancing medical knowledge of the disease is effecting changes in the legal code regarding alcoholics. The Supreme Court decision in Powell vs. Texas indicates that alcoholism will be transferred from the care of correctional authorities to health agencies. Unfortunately, these facilities are unprepared to receive the large number of alcoholics. In a Supreme Court decision, Justice White affirms that a chronic alcoholic, who is publicly intoxicated and can show he was powerless, is protected by the Eighth Amendment. He also states: "The alcoholic is like a person with smallpox who could be convicted for being on the street but not for being ill; or like the epileptic, punishable for driving a car but not for his disease."

Alcoholism is a disease when it causes certain durable symptoms of disorders of a mental, affective, and bodily nature. We are not dealing here with the unspeakable hangover after a night of carousing, but with the gravest consequences which arise in a person due to prolonged overindulgence in alcohol. These disorders are of a mental nature in depression, anxiety, self-accusations, inferiority feelings, character troubles, memory disturbances; of a nervous disorder in equilibrium, neuritis, tremors; of a bodily disorder in lesions of liver, kidneys, heart and arteries, brain damage; of a mixed order as the mental and nervous troubles aggravate general health; and of a spiritual order in the stagnation of spiritual growth.

Of course, *all* these disorders need not be present in order to establish that a person has the disease. They present an overall picture of the progression of the disease in its developing stages. One does not have to wait until one is disabled by the disease in its tragic chronic stages for the admission: "I am an alcoholic." Still, there are many alcoholics who fight the battle of admission until admission becomes a life or death decision. Fortunately, there are many in AA who come to the vital understanding of on-going gradual suicide before the more dire stages of the disease set in.

Doctor Marvin Block, assistant clinical professor of medicine at the State University of New York at Buffalo, points to a major change in the medical attitude toward alcoholism. This is the recognition that alcohol is a drug and that dependence on it is a form of addiction. The drinking of alcohol soon makes this drinker a chemically dependent person. It is a drug addiction open only to some drinkers.

Alcoholics, who begin to suspect the reality of their disease symptoms, and those who newly admit that they have the disease, are frequently given to probings into how they got that way: was it all due to their heredity, their environment, their family, their work, a neurosis, whatever? AA counsels them to keep it simple, to concentrate on this every day of their lives. They can stir up anxieties in their search for *causes* of their illness and find themselves back with their old tranquilizer. It is best that they get to work, seek proper help — *stop the most apparent cause of their illness, their drinking* — and step by step, day by day, begin to put their life together. What is all important is the task of getting a clear mind, unfogged by alcohol, to think and do recovery.

Loss of Control in Drinking — Our American Alcoholics

It is now known that alcoholism appears in a variety of forms in its psychological and physical symptoms amidst the various conditionings of social cultures in Anglo-Saxons, Scandinavians, Latins, American Indians, Blacks, and other ethnic groups. For example, Dr. E.M. Jellinek, in his celebrated book *The Disease Concept of Alcoholism,* observes that a large proportion of French drinkers may incur some damage of chronic alcoholism or develop addiction without their having ever shown intoxication except at certain celebrations. It is also peculiar to the French male alcoholic that he shows no guilt feeling about drinking to his father, brother, or sons, and the male sex in general, but he does show marked guilt toward his mother, wife, daughter, and the female sex in general for his condition. On the other hand, here in America and the Anglo-

Saxon culture in general, frequent intoxication is heavily involved with drink-guilt feelings in both sexes.

On the American scene, the alcoholic-type most commonly evidenced in the AA fellowships is, as Jellinek calls it by the technical name, "gamma alcoholism." This type of alcoholism is characterized by both loss of control over drinking (which, however, does not cancel out the ability to abstain), and physical dependence on drink (with withdrawal symptoms caused by both psychological and physiological processes). Loss of control denotes that stage in the development of drinking when the taking of a drink sets off a chain reaction of drinks. This is sometimes done consciously against the drinker's reasonable will and even with disgust for himself or herself in drinking.

As loss of control progresses, undisciplined drinking takes over, in which the drinker transgresses the rules of society relating to amounts, times, occasions, and locales of drinking. Gradually, the ability to abstain is impaired. Physical dependence on alcohol, "the overpowering desire to drink" in AA language, becomes evident. A physical demand for alcohol is shown in withdrawal symptoms, in the adaptation of cell metabolism, and the drinker's obsessive belief that alcohol in some way relieves him or her. The drinker is now "hooked."

Once freely taken, the drink now takes over the drinker. The drink so masters the drinker that even after years of abstinence, he or she cannot regain control over drinking. Still the drinker can abstain — which is important for the alcoholic who really wants to recover, to be alive. The alcohol-dependent person, the addict, cannot drink normally. This pertains not only to "the heavy stuff" but also to beer and wine. The alcoholic becomes sick when he or she drinks. Try it, you won't like it. It will, however, keep on happening to you in ever-worsening ways. How we alcoholics try to dodge this label, until we come honestly to understand recovery is vitally valuable for us.

Mental compulsions and physical addiction are powerfully activated when the alcoholic drinks. It is not simply a matter of a good person turning into a bad person — and becoming a good person again in recovery who can drink socially again. How can you erase addiction and its complexity of ills, mental, spiritual and social, from a human life? Stop the poisons of alcohol and alcoholic thinking and feeling, which in AA understanding involves a tangle of character defects that repress and frustrate an otherwise healthy ego. This calls for a total life re-formation. We only stop our game of Russian roulette with a bottle when we also stop playing the bad emotional games that lead us to uncork the bottle that springs our addiction. Recovery from so complex a disease has got to be total and, as AA insists, kept as simple as possible step by step, every twenty-four hours. We shall stress this approach in our chapters on the AA Steps of recovery.

There is a milieu of therapies — medical, psychological, spiritual, social — that should team together in arresting the disease of alcoholism. AA is the response of alcoholics themselves recovering who came together in fellowship in a life-style effort to motivate and maintain sobriety. Once the disease is activated, it is ours for life. Continuing recovery for most of us is best attested to by stepping into the AA action of helping one another, and thereby ourselves in the approach of the *risks and challenges of life* for the alcoholic.

There is nothing so very different about all this, since life is a risk and a challenge for everyone, and people do need one another! Life has special problems for certain people and alcoholics in Alcoholics Anonymous' shared experiences have come a long way in this learning-experience. There are some two hundred kindred therapies that have learned from the model experience of AA in alcoholic recovery all the way from drug therapies to Gamblers Anonymous.

Alcohol Addiction

In the fast-rising tide of drug addiction in America today, especially amongst our youth, we are prone to imagine the addict as a long-haired youth mainlining with heroin or popping pills. We find it shocking to know that the most prevalent form of drug addiction is among youths, in the form of addiction to alcohol. More and more young people are coming into AA.

For most drinkers, alcohol is no more than a beverage which serves to relax the drinker. Actually, for alcoholics, it is a drug that addicts them. This is the disease of alcohol addiction. Contrary to popular belief, excessive drinking is not the distinguishing symptom of the disease. Jellinek pointed out *the distinguishing symptom is the loss of control over drinking.* In AA language, these people are powerless over alcohol. They do not step up to the bar, they rush to it like the charge of the light brigade. Their lives have become unmanageable.

This dysfunction involves psychological and physical disorders. Withdrawal shows these disorders in mental and bodily drives for the drug. The start of recovery is far more than the pledge, no matter how solemn, "never to drink again" mouthed during the pangs of a hangover. We do not instantly step out of the mess any more than we instantly step into it. It is perhaps overly stated by some older alcoholics that alcoholism takes many years of practice before it takes on the form of addiction. The speed of youth today in the total drug scene is bringing teenagers into AA with scarey case histories that match those of old-timers with many years of practice. Now that we are learning more about the diseased, we are learning more about the disease. Still, there is far more research required to acquire an adequate picture of alcoholism in our times.

Ethyl alcohol is a drug. The World Health Organization's Expert Committee on Alcohol in 1954 stated: "Alcohol must be considered a drug whose pharmacological action is intermediate in kind and degree between addiction-producing and habit-forming drugs, so that compulsive craving and dependence can develop in those individuals whose makeup leads them to seek and find an escape in alcohol." It is now clear that following discontinuation of alcohol after a prolonged period of very heavy drinking, severe withdrawal symptoms,

29

which in a limited number of cases include convulsions or delirium or both, may occur. These latter symptoms are more dangerous to the life of the individual than any of the manifestations of withdrawal of morphine. When serious symptoms follow the withdrawal of alcohol, they persist almost as long as do those following the withdrawal of opiates.

There can be no doubt that acute cases of chronic alcoholism need specialized medical supervision for the discontinuation of alcohol. On the human level, AA people, who have themselves undergone severe withdrawals, are real Godsends to fellow alcoholics in these dire straits. Particularly, they are knowledgeable enough to know that just any doctor will not do, but a doctor who understands alcoholics. Unfortunately, there are too many physicians who either can't be bothered or are not equipped with the know-how in treating alcoholics.

Popping the X Factor

"How did I get this way? I know a lot of heavy drinkers who did not get into this mess. Where did I go wrong? Or did I go wrong? Was I wrong from the start because of an alcoholic heredity? Or did my environment make me do it?

We have already spoken of the alcoholic's puzzlement about the causes of his or her disease. The problem needs more consideration because it comes back again and again to the drinking alcoholic and the alcoholic in recovery. It is echoed by significant others, especially as they witness the drinking alcoholic drink on, even against his or her reasonable will.

Experts in the field of alcohol studies have no formula, no neat categorical judgment that expresses *the cause* or *the causes* of alcoholism. It is an X factor or X factors to date unknown. When we focus on what Jellinek calls the distinguishing symptom of alcoholism, the loss of control in drinking, we have no one undisputed answer why this occurs in some drinkers who are alcoholics. Is the cause found in a psychological disorder? Is it a compulsion rooted in a mental pathology? Or is it a physical disorder? Could it be caused by acquired modes of living, say in acquired nutritional habits? The fact that the loss of control does not occur in a large group of excessive drinkers seems to point to a predisposing X factor or factors, say, in a person's genetic pattern. To date, we have no certain answer.

When the X factor is popped, the alcoholic is powerless over alcohol. The human brain, the computer center of the chemical plant of our body, goes into a "loop" reaction. In-put signals from various functions of body to brain, and out-put signals from brain to body functions and "fail-safe" circuits, which trigger alarm warnings to go wacky. Proper controls are wanting for the chemicals, Seratonin for sleep, Neopenephrin for digestion, Noradrenalin for defense mechanisms. This drinker, instead of feeling drowsy, is wide awake with no nausea and feels that he can do anything and, while in this euphoria, consumes more alcohol. Harry is the life of the party. Harriet is a real go-go girl.

As the disease progresses, the opposite effects unpredictably set in: sudden deep sleep, nausea, and depression. As long as the addict imbibes the drug, these unmanageable conditions will endure. It all begins with the first drink. Hard to understand? Certainly it is, because 80 percent of drinkers do not experience this "loop" reaction. When the ordinary drinker indulges, alarm bells go off in the brain. Body chemistry responds normally. "Wow, I don't want that scene again. It costs me." And he or she means just that! But this is not the way for the alcoholic who pops his or her X factor, whatever it is that causes alcoholism. The alcoholic characteristically denies that it is really that bad and dodges the responsibility of moderate drinking.

There are alcoholics who give more time to speculating why they drink, and search out the latest book on alcoholism in the hope of finding out "what caused it," with high expectations of discovering some pill to end it, rather than honestly facing their day by day personal homework for recovery. There is sufficient scientific evidence for arresting the disease and sufficient AA experience in "growing up" in a recovering life-style. Good medicine is important to get a person through the physical pangs of withdrawal, to arrest a bad liver or whatever; the knowledge and skill of psychology is important to overcome the alcoholic's frustration neurosis; but more than these a life-style motivation and maintenance and total sobriety in a life worth living is the over-all need for recovery. For if the victim of the disease of alcoholism drink again, the disease will certainly progress onward with more grievous tragic effects. For many recovering alcoholics, AA is the answer to this life-style need.

It is a source of amazement for this writer that some experts in alcohol studies misunderstand the vital value of the AA fellowship. They seem perplexed by the fact that laymen, non-professionals, unschooled in the complex field of alcohol studies can contribute vitally to alcoholic recovery. They find the vocabulary of AA ambiguous. They suspect the AA approach overly modelled on one's personal recovery too emotional, and the use of a moral therapy in arresting a disease some find terribly unscientific.

All of this moves these experts to question AA recoveries. What is more amazing, however, is their own lack of an empirical understanding of AA and the fact that they are rather emotional about some of their experiences with some AA people. Could it be that they met the wrong AA's or had the wrong pre-conceived ideas about what they were going to experience? It is hoped that this book can at least urge them to re-examine their understanding. This complex disease requires a team, a complex of healing helpers for recovery: medical, psychological, spiritual, social, and above all, the self-help of the diseased in recovery fellowship.

III.   STAGES OF THE DISEASE

At the punch bowl's brink
Let the thirsty think
What they say in Japan,
"First the man takes a drink
Then the drink takes a drink,
Then the drink takes the man."
Adage from the Orient.

The first use of alcoholic beverages is generally a matter of curiosity mingled with social motivation. Alcohol drinking has a lively social symbolism. The man with a drink can feel more manly in his group, and today's woman can experience more liberation in libation. In contrast to the average social drinker, however, the prospective alcoholic soon experiences a rewarding relief, a zoom feeling, from drinking. At first, one is more or less prone to identify this relief, this "high," with the social situation rather than with the drinking. One likes the good fellowship, the escape from the dull routine of the day.

Sooner or later, there is awareness of the relation between drinking and relief, "the precious high times." "Relief" is a curious word that covers a variety of moods and modes of living in each one of us. For some, it means a soft, tranquil feeling; for others it means a blast-off of energy.

The feeling of relief is the most important thing to the prospective alcoholic. Either because tensions for the prospective alcoholic are greater than for others, or because the prospective alcoholic is not well equipped emotionally to handle tension. AA stories reveal such patterns of behavior.

The Preparatory Stage

At the beginning of the drinking career in the prospective alcoholic, "relief-drinking" is only sought occasionally but, in a matter of time, it could be six months or two years, tolerance for tension decreases. Drinking relief is sought daily. Still there may be no occasions of intoxication. The drinker considers himself or herself following the rather ordinary American custom of drinking toward the end of the day. But the prospective alcoholic desires more and more during the relaxing evenings, and they come to involve heavy drinking in comparison with others in one's circle. Still, the drinking may not be conspicuous to the drinker or to others. "Charlie can take it." "Ann is a lively one."

An increase of alcohol tolerance gradually becomes noticeable. This drinker is requiring more and more to get relaxed. The glass crutch is beginning to show. Relaxation is coming to mean intoxication, although to this drinker it just means feeling "high." These are danger signals that could be announcing the onset of the disease. They are unhealthy symptoms. The drinker is gradually getting the message that his or her life is becoming physically and morally unbalanced. Drinking is getting too much priority. However, the matter is not given too much concern. "Don't bother me; I can cope."

The twilight zone between the preparatory stage and the onset of the disease is dawning. Signs of a progressive decrease in the ability of the digestive and nervous system to tolerate alcohol are surfacing. But the drinker does not really want to recognize them. They are camouflaged by a variety of alibis and dodges. "Of course, we all pay a price for a happy time." "I drink a little more than you because I've had a rough day. I need to unwind." Or "I'm a fast moving free spirit. Don't fence me in." "This is the only way to swing a deal. Get a glow on." This prospective alcoholic refuses to face the reality: "I am starting to drink too much for my own good."

The first to feel the impact of this sorry situation is usually the drinker's family. A concerned spouse, a parent, may try to bring home to him or her the growing impulse of gulping drinks, taking drinks before a party or appointment. The prospective alcoholic promises to check it, but time and again these promises prove to be more alibis to silence the truth. Some spouses and parents at this stage are real helpmates toward recovery, not by going it alone on their own resources, not by nagging talks or pious moralizing, but by seeking knowledgeable aid medically and by going to Al-Anon. Al-Anon is part of our local AA fellowship in supporting service to the troubled family of the alcoholic and also the prospective alcoholic. Usually, the prospective alcoholic will not seek help because he or she wants to believe that his or her problem is not that serious.

The Setting-In of the Disease

By now, it is evident that we are dealing with the birth pangs of alcoholism. Intoxications are disturbing an otherwise manageable life. "Alcoholic thinking and feeling" are settling into the drinker's life. There is great preoccupation with the need for a drink. There is real concern about adequate supply at a party or luncheon. Will one's impulsive drinking be noticed? Guilt feelings develop about one's drinking behavior, but nothing is really done to correct them. Heavy drinking is increasing for the sake of emotional anesthesia, which is really a narcosis — a numbing that fades into oblivion.

The drinker tries to make excuses. He or she is just trying to get a "glow on," trying to get a bit "high" out of the lows. Actually, this drinker is drinking to get drunk. Often the drinker is at first unaware of this fact. The drinker will not honestly admit that he or she wants intoxication.

The memory blank-out is a scarey experience for many of us. "Did I drive the car home last night? Is it in good condition? Was I all right when we left the party?" Non-addictive drinkers may also experience these losses of memory, but only infrequently and after heavy intoxication. The prospective alcoholic experiences these disturbances more and more often as he or she advances into the disease. The causes of the memory blank-outs are not known. They may be due to malutilization of oxygen. For some drinkers, this temporary impairment of memory and the general threat of alcoholism to their welfare serve as a bottoming out of their alcoholic folly, and they seek recovery through the AA program. Frequently they are assisted in this move by a former drinking companion who had similar experiences and joined the AA fellowship for a recovery life-style. A good medical examination by a knowledgeable physician should be had at this point, with the honest admission of one's drinking history.

By now, it should be plainly evident to the drinker that he or she is an alcoholic, at least in the setting-in of the disease which is technically called the prodromal stage. The step over the line into the disease is not easily clocked. This drinker is not using alcohol as a beverage but as a drug that the drinker needs. This style of drinking is very different from the ordinary social drinker. For this reason, drinking becomes more and more surreptitious, concealed, so that amounts are not known to others — as if this is possible!

In the whole history of the problem drinker described in these stages, he or she can be called "alcoholic" inasmuch as the drinker is harming life, one's own and those around him or her. As this label is applied to a person, however, it gives rise to deep-seated resentments. It is a sort of taboo for the drinking alcoholic because it tells him or her about an identity the drinker does not want to admit. It tells them they are sick people, and indeed they are so long as they drink.

After physical recovery from an intoxication, the confirmed drinker returns to another bout in a matter of time. In this onset stage, he or she is not homing to the drink out of uncontrollable compulsion but out of psychological conflicts and/or due to social situations involving drinking. Alcoholic anxieties look for the old tranquilizer. Presence at a drinking party, a businessman's wet luncheon, among the jolly crowd at the bar — all contribute toward setting the alcoholic on his or her merry-go-round that will eventually be a dizzy trip to pain and guilt-laden sorrow. The cocktail party and commuter-bar atmosphere, drinking while standing, gulping drinks, with the barest minimum of food, are highly favorable for reactivating the illness.

This drinker could say "no" to the first drink but he or she lacks the real urge and often the knowledgeable support to do so. Too often people who want to help unwittingly say the wrong things. How do you get to an alcoholic? There are people who know out of their own vital gut-level experience. Here is the real forte of the AA approach.

Alcoholics are never "policed" away from their cups, never forced. They must eventually come to want recovery meaningfully, free from the alcoholic's perspective, his or her way of looking at life from inside a glass cage, if recovery is to begin at all.

Still, as every alcoholic knows, there is always some tiny bit of the drive to recover, some ray of hope. It could be the spark awaiting to be kindled. AA people, from their own experience are knowledgeable in recognizing that spark, and cultivating it in the AA Steps of recovery. Our own stories relate our resistance to recovery and how we overcame the mess. We can identify because we have been there in the pits and made it to recovery.

Why does this kind of drinker return to drinking after so many repeated tragedies? How difficult this is for the sober majority to understand! Although the alcoholic will not admit it, he or she has come to the belief that will-power is gone. In the onset of the disease this consciousness is starting to settle into the alcoholic's life after repeated failures to drink socially. There is a search to regain self-control, not by stopping the drinking, but through an effort to control the amount of drinking. The alcoholic does not really understand what the lessening of control in drinking means. It is looked upon as a matter of personal, very private will-power, a fanciful myth for this badly damaged drinker.

In these times of the onset of the disease, intoxications are so overtly conspicuous and repeated that parents, spouse, friends, employer, clergymen make extra effort to get this sick drinker to awaken to his dire condition and to cooperate with a recovery therapy. But the onset of the disease is surfacing a definite loss of self-esteem; neglect of personal appearance is worsening along with response to duties to family and work. Failure to appear at work on Mondays is now moving into

Tuesdays. The housewife's "headaches" are moving out of the Monday blahs into the week. Sometimes the weakening self-esteem is attempted to be compensated for in grandiose behavior such as big spending, or big talk, lavish promises.

Gradually, aggressive behavior increases and the drinker adopts more deep-rooted feelings of resentment, a sense of isolation from others. Frustration neurosis is becoming a way of life. People do not understand. Friends are dropped. Jobs are changed. The whole family is in an emotional mish-mash. Spouse and children may enjoy good social activities but now they are withdrawing out of embarrassment or they may seek to escape the home environment through outside activities. All of this only intensifies the drinker's isolation and resentments. He or she indulges in self-pity, which sometimes softens a family to solace the poor beknighted alcoholic. These are emotional games alcoholics play and they need experienced handling. Al-Anon can give profitable counsel in these perplexing times for a family. More often the alcoholic has to be told that the family can take no more of this nightmare. This is often misunderstood as a form of mental cruelty by the sober majority. There are ways of bringing home this message, however, which amount to a meaningful message rather than just a nagging talk that the alcoholic knows is just "talk."

The family gets the message that they are no longer talking to a person who listens, but a person who is stepping into drug addiction, if he or she is not already there. This alcoholic is thinking about the next drink. Alcohol is a food, depressant, and anesthetic. It is a drug that addicts some people, even though distillers prefer to advertise it only as a beverage. It can substitute for food, to some extent, for the body is getting calories in drinking. This substitution is a danger for alcoholics. They get enough calories not to want foods which supply the vitamins, proteins and minerals that their bodies need for good health. Neglect of proper nutrition aggravates the effects of heavy drinking on the body. Frequently the alcoholic is hospitalized in his or her run-down condition. The family or friends of the alcoholic should not fall victims to his or her personal shame or the social taboos of alcoholism. The facts of the alcoholic's drinking history should be plainly told to the doctor.

Another of the common organic effects of alcoholism is the decrease of the sexual drive. This increases hostility in one's spouse. But even when the impotence is absent, the spouse is so personally disgusted at the alcoholic's bodily and moral condition that love and affection are dampened or even turned off. The alcoholic is not fit to sleep with or to have in the same room. Many valiant spouses endure this situation for many years for the sake of the children, but when the confirmed drinker persists in obstinacy, many spouses seek divorce or at least separation.

Chronic Stage

It is difficult to draw a thin line between the onset and the break-through of this subtle disease. In time, the drinker becomes very conscious of the fact that he or she is not dealing with a transitory and easily remedied illness. The illness, psychological and physical, has settled in the alcoholic's life. The chronic stage has arrived with all its acute symptoms of enduring disturbance.

On the interpersonal level, the alcoholic increases in fear of establishing meaningful relationships, has low frustration tolerance, and greater need for controls and dependency. By now, resentments, the conflict between the alcoholic's needs and personal duties, loss of self-esteem, doubts and false promises have so disorganized the addict's life that he or she cannot start the day without a drink. Drinking is a way of life. It is the time of "the benders," the prolonged intoxications with their characteristic moral and physical deterioration.

Alcoholic psychosis may occur at this time, which claims ten percent of alcoholics. DT's, or delirium tremens, account for 37 percent of all cases of alcoholic psychosis. The victim "sees" things, usually animals, and shakes uncontrollably. The drinker in the chronic stage experiences a bottoming of self-esteem and does not care with whom he or she drinks. Commercial products, such as rubbing alcohol, even perfumes, may be ingested when it is impossible to get a drink. You don't believe this? Deprive a chronic alcoholic and become a believer!

There is a loss of tolerance for alcohol at this time. A stuporous state is caused by half the number of drinks formerly required. Anxiety, indefinable fears and tremors, occur as soon as alcohol intake stops, and so the drinker continues drinking "to keep going." Underlying symptoms of a personality disorder now intensify into an obsessive character. Rationalizations become weaker and in some cases confused religious desires "to be saved" develop. The addict is really hitting the bottom of the pit. Yet, notwithstanding all these grave ills, some alcoholics still remain opposed to therapy. Dr. Karl Menninger argues that alcoholism is based on impulses of self-destruction and guilt.

The option should be clear to the chronic alcoholic that he or she either seeks help to recover or goes insane or dies. In the past, many came to AA in such a low-bottom crisis. As knowledge and education about the disease increases, more and more alcoholics do not wait for the extreme crisis. They know what is ahead of them if they continue drinking. Many do not wait for the big fall-out. In our times, we are better informed about the progression of the disease. Still, too many wait unnecessarily long in the developing crisis. Clinical experience shows that this crisis-awakening of what is going on and what is to come in the drinking alcoholic's life, can be induced by knowledgeable help. Of course, it is another matter to maintain it as a life-style. Too many people are allowed to leave clinical care with the impression that their nightmare is over and even believe that they are "cured." In fact, they are sometimes assured by people, who ought to know better, that they are "cured" and can be social drinkers. Even in the early stages, the prospective alcoholic can be intercepted. However, much remains to be done in the study of this condition.

Hospital care can never be the last word but only the beginning in the recovery process of the alcoholic. In some communities, hospital care, unfortunately, cannot even be dignified as a stage in recovery. This writer has personal experience as a volunteer counselor in a large city hosptal in which alcoholics of the inner city poor are indiscriminately thrown in with mental patients, where it is easily possible for them to drink during their hospitalization, and which proved to be little more than a lock-up situation with some medication to ease physical pain. Psychiatric help is minimal in the over-crowded conditions and overworked staff. This community has "alcoholic recovery therapy" as a part of its public health service. This example of the facade of recovery therapy is by no means exceptional, especially in our large cities. Who is to blame? It is part of our over-all calloused indifference to the number one health problem in the nation. People don't like to be bothered about alcoholism.

Alcoholism is a progressive disease. It is a disease in itself and symptomatic of various other disorders, physical and psychological. From this introductory picture, understanding should be poignantly brought home to us of the characteristic symptom of the disease in the *addict's loss of control in drinking,* which affects the total person in the abnormalities of alcoholic behavior and reaches beyond the drinker with tragic consequences to family and society.

It should be understood that the treatment of the disease requires a variety of disciplines as an illness of the body, a personality disorder, a disease that disrupts economic life and society. The moral *dis-ease* of the spiritual decline of the person is of special concern to religion. Understanding the process of recovery of so insidious a total disease requires more than restoration to bodily health, more than taking medication, more than organizing human behavior. It means a real building of the human; a new, continuing life-perspective and lifestyle to motivate and maintain sobriety in a worthwhile life.

Alcoholics Anonymous was initiated in response to this need.

IV. THE PERSON WHO HAS ALCOHOLISM

The alcoholic has lost the power of choice in the matter
of drinking and this is precisely the nature of his disease.
Marty Mann, Primer on Alcoholism

To understand alcoholic recovery we must focus on understanding the person who is alcoholic. This is especially true
since the disease of alcoholism involves the total person and is
not just a bodily ailment. As a disease, it envelops a human life
and gradually dehumanizes it, not only by defacing human
appearance but by degrading human perspectives, behavior,
and values. This is a disease that progresses in stages of
depersonalization in the making of the chemically dependent
person.

Alcoholic People: The Drinking-Sick
The Recovering

We have been talking about the dark side of the alcoholic's
life-picture. But it need not be the total picture, even though
this disease is for life. There need not be a continuing
actualization of the disease. There can be a self-actualization, a
re-birth of the integral person, a man, a woman, alive to life
rather than chemical dependency on a substance called ethyl
alcohol.

This disease can be arrested in its life-destroying power, it
can be controlled so that a human being can be open again to
the joy of living, to human dignity. This is the bright side of the
alcoholic's life-picture. I say "alcoholic" because this person still
has the disease for life, once he or she is diagnosed positively.
The recovering *and recovered* alcoholic is not a cured person,
an ex-alcoholic; he or she is an ex-drunk, to be sure, but not
an ex-alcoholic. The disease can be reactivated by drinking
again. Denial, a rugged psychological symptom of the disease,

43

must be arrested by vital remembrance: "I am an alcoholic!" Of course the "I" for a person is always more central than any of our label-identities, and our culture has a nasty habit of identifying by labels. The recovered life of the alcoholic person develops into channels of personal initiative that unlock depths and heights of human goodness, the grandeur and the beauty of the art of purposeful living. And it is all so simply real, so plainly human.

Authentic recovery never travels the route of the sentimental gush of a problem-free utopia. The recovered has learned to cope with vital problems and, what is more, to use them to his or her advantage in a spirit of gratitude and hope. Is it so strange that alcoholics in recovery and the *recovered* should come together in a fellowship to share the blessings of this human awakening so needed in this world?

Understanding alcoholic recovery in any realistic sense demands more than understanding what the disease does to a person. It demands that *we think positively what recovery can do for a person*. We are so used to stereotyping the alcoholic in the one dark dimension of the sick person, even the traditionally overworked image of the Skid Row bum, that it is difficult for many to use the label "alcoholic" outside this context. We fail to come to an understanding that a recovering alcoholic can also be a fellow human, even a sterling example of virtue. In many walks of life, AA people show this to be true. I am speaking here of the large percentage of the fellowship that honestly follow the program over the years, one day at a time. As in any membership, there is more to belonging than vocal identity.

In the past, when we spoke of the alcoholic, we conjured up the image of a drunkard, a disreputable sot, a flaky lush practically life-committed to his or her cups. This image endures in our times, although attitudes are changing. Alcoholics Anonymous and the National Council on Alcoholism and public health agencies are greatly responsible for burying this bias. The thousands of recovering alcoholics in communities in every state attest this fact. Unfortunately, dictionaries have not yet caught up with the new meaning of the word "alcoholic" signifying not only the drinking sick alcoholic but also the recovering and the *recovered*. This is more than a case of word-play or semantics. We are talking about a word packed with emotional power that can be a character label either for good or bad, depending on one's realistic understanding. The person who is alcoholic can be drinking-sick, even if recovering.

In our present age, the recovery of many thousands of alcoholics is a hopeful breakthrough from the dismal history of the disease in the past. In our era of increasing permissiveness, marked by the explosion of the total drug scene, it is comforting to know that many are succeeding in a physical and moral (not moralizing) recovery from the most widespread drug addiction known to Western man.

People have become anxiety-laden about the general crisis of human welfare in these times of earth-pollution and the inward pollution of human life. In the area of alcoholism, notwithstanding the increase in the wet-set, particularly among our youth, there is real hope for recovery. It is hope sprung not only from laboratory techniques of treatment. More than that, it is a living personal hope communicated by recovering and *recovered* alcoholics in the fellowship of AA groups to fellow sufferers, that they too can stop drinking and really learn that alcohol is not needed in a total life reformation.

What Sort of Person Gets Alcoholism?

The question is phrased this way because we are not so much concerned here with the fuzzy question of remote predispositions to alcoholism in heredity, but rather with the kind of person who is disposed to stepping into the disease. Stepping out of the activation of the disease must take careful note of how the drinker in life was set up to step into it. Professionals in the various fields of alcohol studies are prone to charter the alcoholic's route into alcoholism in its various types according to their particular discipline.

45

The psychologist stresses the behavioral course of the disease. The pharmacologist focuses on the drug properties of ethyl alcohol and how they affect certain people. The physiologist charts the stages of bodily debilitation. Experts in social studies preempt the societal conditionings. Clergy look at the spiritual decline. All these disciplines contribute to important insights in understanding the disease. Any workable model of recovery must take all these factors into account. They contribute to putting together again the Humpty-Dumpty life of the alcoholic person. Of course, the life-style art of keeping an alcoholic life together in terms of his or her personal living outside of a controlled therapeutic community of a hospital or sanatorium is another story. Dare we propose "controlled drinking" for the addicted?

Getting alcoholism is, of course, not the same for everyone, because "alcoholic" is a word covering varied types of alcoholics. Broadly speaking, the alcoholic is anyone who harms himself and others by drinking alcoholic beverages. Our concern in this book, as was initially stated, is with persons afflicted with the disease of alcoholism, the chronic alcoholics of the gamma type, described in the preceding chapter. However, it is important to take into account two broad categories, the reactive or neurotic alcoholic and the addicted, because differentiation between the two groups is not always clear.

Reactive or neurotic alcoholics have relatively normal prealcoholic personality structures and reasonable adjustment in the family, education, work, and society in general. These persons use alcohol to excess when in a stress situation of unusually long duration. An episode of excessive drinking has a determinable onset, develops in a course of tension release, and may terminate through some measure of control exercised by the individual. But some reactive alcoholics become so enmeshed in their neurotic drinking that they regress to a state approximating the chronic state of the disease.

The alcohol addict has a somewhat different development. He grows out of personality disorders in his pre-alcoholic history. There are difficulties in adjustment in family life, in school, at work, in attempts at marital love and affection. In AA language, "drinking did not make me into the man I was. But the man I was made me a drunkard." It is evident that all persons with personality disorders do not become alcoholics. Why some people do, is to date unexplained.

One cannot clearly point to exactly when addiction settles into a life. There is sometimes a low degree of observable external stress associated with the onset of a drinking episode. Needs for drinking are largely internal and to the sober majority do not seem to make sense. Drinking bouts usually continue into sickness. The drinker is searching for "an escape," usually out of unconscious drives. The alcoholic does not really know what is happening to him or her. There is a deprivation in some way of a significant emotional relationship that is traceable to one's early life, perhaps in the death of a parent, or emotional or physical absence of a parent. Some addicted alcoholics are the children of overly protective or indulgent mothers, others of psychotic mothers, or a parent severely alcoholic during one's childhood years. Others come from religiously abstinent families, where a one-sided fear of "demon drink" prevailed.

AA stories not infrequently tell of other life histories where none of the above cited crises are present. These reveal growing up in normal households, in happy childhoods. Still, personality disorders and emotional immaturities grow into alcoholic crises. There is more going on here than just an escape mechanism. There is a search for a way of getting spirited from the spirits. How sadly true that the experience is dispiriting. Alcohol is a depressant drug.

Alcoholic depression is a mixed bag of psychological, physical, and social causes. Severe loneliness and emptiness result in the use of the alcoholic's characteristic defense mechanism, denial. It is an inbuilt attitude of a frustration neurosis. This drinking alcoholic denies that he or she is alcoholic. When confronted, how often we hear the response: "I can stop any time I want to." This is the denial of loss of control. Denial becomes a way of living: denial of inferiority, denial of loss of self-respect, denial of depression, denial of dependence on the chemical. More often, angry denials are internalized and one attempts to consume them in drink. "Drown out your sorrows." One can hardly simply localize this as an oral perversion. It is the perversion of a total life.

There is great danger in diagnosing oneself, in trying to understand oneself as alcoholic, in taking any one model of the alcoholic too literally. Experts are sometimes mistaken in understanding a patient's kind of alcoholic identity. People have their own way of being unique, and this calls for knowledgeable flexibility in treatment. No books can possibly handle all ground rules here. The understanding of an alcoholic must center on a living person rather than an abstract model. The model can, of course, be a useful tool.

The expression paraphrased by many recovering alcoholics in AA groups might be gainfully attended to by therapists: "Here I am accepted as an important *person*." As Dr. Morris E. Chafetz, Director of the National Institute on Alcohol Abuse and Alcoholism, in *Frontiers of Alcoholism* points out concerning the psychotherapist in treating alcoholics:

> Fundamentally he must be a warm, kind, interested individual who can at the same time set and maintain reality-oriented limits; he must not and cannot assume moralizing and punitive attitudes. Since we are dealing with a disorder of early personality development, words are of little use; *it is not what we say to the alcoholic, but what we really feel* and do that will determine the outcome. Alcoholism as a preverbal disorder, must be treated by action — by "doing for" the patient.

One Out of Ten Drinkers

The myth of alcoholism as a Skid Row disease dies hard. We are prone to imagine the alcoholic in the worst possible way, in the final symptoms of the disease, and in the worst possible surroundings. Actually only a small percentage of Skid Row is alcoholic. One out of ten of our 100 million drinking population has alcoholism. (Jellinek maintained that the proportion of alcoholics, addictive and non-addictive, varies from country to country, but *does not seem to exceed five or six percent* of all users of alcoholic beverages.) The vast majority are far distant from the tawdry alleys of Skid Row. They are among the affluent, the middle class. Many are successful, business-wise. Many are intelligent, sensitive men and women. It is estimated that twenty percent of the total population in America suffers *some* damage from their misuses of alcoholic drinking.

For the most part, addictive alcoholics are regularly employed in industry and the professions. As the disease progresses they have high rates of absenteeism, and among workers they also have high accident rates. In teamwork or assembly line work, they have a deteriorating effect on morale. Industry is learning the need to spot the alcoholic, both in shop and office, and to require him or her to have proper therapy.

Housewives compose a growing number of "concealed alcoholics," progressing in their disease before their families realize the gravity of their illness. How surprised many of the sober majority really are, when the alcoholic is uncovered, a person with an otherwise good name, from a good family, in a good neighborhood. It is almost as if we expected the discovery to take place beneath a heap of newspapers in a dark alley on Skid Row! This sickness can strike anywhere. Who are the immune?

Unfortunately, doctors are often ill prepared to understand and treat the alcoholic. Dr. Morris E. Chafetz comments: "Medical students receive virtually no training in medical schools on alcoholism, because their teachers, the older doctors, usually have the stereotyped image of alcoholics as the Skid-Row type, and this just isn't true in most cases." More younger doctors, fortunately, are awakening to the urgent need of the informed and understanding physician.

A current study of the American drinker was undertaken at George Washington University, Washington, D.C. The study found that 68% of Americans drink and 13% drink heavily. Studies on the drinking habits of Americans, such as Dr.

Cahalan's researches, are still in their beginnings, and more research is needed to come up with an over-all picture in detail.

What sort of traits constitute the alcoholic personality? It is possible to give a character picture of the sick-drinking alcoholic. Unfortunately, people expect to find them in any one alcoholic. The sick-drinking alcoholic is really not an attractive personality. Deep depressions, aggressions, resentments, guilt-feelings, alienations, and fears develop. They constitute sources for continued drinking. They do not simply go away in recovery by the alcoholic stopping his or her drinking. They are in need of treatment by reformation of attitudes, habits, and life-style. Recovery means not only recovery from excessive drinking, but also from these unhealthy character traits.

However, over-all studies of alcoholics show there is not any specific personality trait or physical characteristic that inevitably leads to excessive drinking. The alcoholic commonly has a low capacity for coping with tensions, an emotional state of omnipotence — doing and accomplishing in a hurry, wanting what one wants, when one wants it, the way one wants it — ungrateful for what one receives; all of which lead to further frustrations. They are more or less present in the alcoholic before his or her drinking career. Yet there are many people with pronounced emotional immaturity who do not turn to alcohol. We have no way of foretelling who will become alcoholic.

The Riddle of the Weak-Willed Drinker

People generally regard the alcoholic as a weak-willed drinker, that the alcoholic loses strength of will to moderate or stop his or her drinking once the drinking gets under way. Yet at the same time, the alcoholic drinker has a strong will not to change this excessive drinking behavior. The alcoholic strongly resists giving up this drinking career. Therapy for recovery is either avoided or not co-operated with by strong-willed denials

50

by the alcoholic that he or she does not need it, does not want it. And this is true of a large percentage of alcoholics, who continue to resist any form of treatment for alcoholism. Thus we have the riddle of the weak-willed, strong-willed alcoholic.

Among the types of interpersonal behavior patterns, alcoholics appear to be the bossy-managerial type of person. In their drinking careers, they want to boss and manage their own life, to drink, to do their thing. They want what they want, and they want it, with a kind of omnipotence. Of course, it is a sort of childish, immature tantrum, because they are becoming more and more chemically dependent, and they are being bossed and managed by ethyl alcohol with eventual loss of will power as long as they allow this to happen.

It is difficult to mark the passing of the line where the drinker's drive to drink is not really a decision but an addiction. But, we can recognize it when it has set into a life. It is another way of speaking of the loss of control in drinking by the addicted drinker. How difficult it is for the sober majority to understand this plight of the alcoholic drug addict! For most of us, the use of alcoholic beverages is a form of social drinking, but for the alcoholic it is a drug-trip, once the disease has set in. This alcoholic's drive to drink is no healthy, strong will power, but a sick addiction. There is no real man power here that we sometimes imaginatively associate with the drinking man. Nor is there liberation for the addicted woman. There is a very sick person, a form of enslavement.

In normal drinking together, we find a sign of friendship, "taking in the stream of life," a symbol of identity greater than eating. This deep symbolic meaning of drinking can give rise to "social pressures" to drink, but it is not the reason for the addict's compulsive drinking that wells up out of an addictive body and compulsive spirit. There are also utility functions to normal drinking in many cultures that accept drinking as a way of nourishment and relaxation, "the pause that refreshes," "capping a business transaction with a drink." But the chronic alcoholic does not just drink. He or she addicts himself or herself. Most people stay within culturally accepted drinking

51

behaviors and drink as an expression of their culture. The alcohol addict in drinking makes predominant use of a drug. This kind of drinking is not a product of a culture. It is exceptional.

Particularly in America, we are given easily to the notion that a person can be what he or she wants to be. It is a case of personal liberty, freedom of choice, personal determination, rugged individualism. "Do your thing." We like to opine that the alcoholic is just weak willed and that given a good charge of will power, he or she can pull out of it. It's all a case of do it yourself.

Dr. Morris E. Chafetz, after years of experience in treating alcoholics, remarks: "Doctors seem to have the opinion that alcoholics can help themselves, if they want to. And because people often accept a doctor's own opinion as truth, the problem of alcoholism has not really been understood by enough people. This has to change." How often we recovering alcoholics can recall our own intention to pledge ourselves to sobriety, to cut down on our drinking, to drink as social drinkers. But we could not do it on our own will power, left to our own individual resources. We needed help for genuine, total sobriety. However, it is not all a case of simply getting help. We need help that is really knowledgeable, understanding. There are some physicians and psychotherapists who prove to be of little or no help. There are some who have given up on alcoholics and believe that alcoholics are not motivated for treatment.

There are various attempts to motivate alcohol addicts into moderate drinking. Some of these appear to succeed under controlled laboratory conditions, but when the alcoholic returns to his or her life in the world, the moderate drinking soon turns into intoxication. AA launched the first great constructive effort to correct this myth of inducing moderate drinking as a route for recovery of the alcohol addict. AA also disbelieves in recovery simply by individual will power. There is a long history of failures to support this view.

The Drug and I

Alcoholic beverages have a central place in times of celebration and relaxation. They facilitate social intercourse, enhance the enjoyment of other foods, and require visible activity in the course of consumption. It is not at all surprising that alcoholic beverages became so very much acculturated in man's history and that their acceptance became so complete. However, because their main constituent, alcohol, is a sedative drug, they can be more than gentle inebriants when misused; they have produced and continue to produce great tragedies in human life.

Is the drug misused because of inborn errors of enzyme functioning, or chromosome imbalance in some of us? To date, we don't know. What we do know is that to deal with the loss of control in drinking, the AA program of total abstinence to celebrate healthy living is the most successful therapy. The use of substitute drugs, tranquilizers, anti-depessants, sedatives, protective drugs such as antabuse and temposil, and electric shock treatment may be useful on the way to recovery, but it is the person who is alcoholic who must recover from his or her chemical dependency trip to a life worth living.

Recovery therapy begins with the honest admission by the alcoholic that his or her life is powerless over alcohol and this life is unmanageable. This drinker is an addict to a drug that is properly used by most drinkers. The World Health Organization's Committee on Alcohol and Alcoholism designated ethyl alcohol as a drug "intermediate in kind and degree between habit forming drugs and addiction producing drugs." It leads to addiction in a maximum of ten percent of its users, over a period usually from three to fifteen years of heavy imbibing. However, the time dimension is highly relative as case studies of alcoholics, especially in the speed living of our youth, reveal. These are the addictive alcoholics, who should not drink. Unlike other drugs, alcohol requires less and less amounts to victimize its addicts.

53

What is especially helpful in AA group recovery is that AA people know *drug-addictive thinking and feeling.* They are alcoholics with years of experience in the painful effort to displace muddled rationalizations with proper understanding of what recovery means. "Really we are not too weak to abstain," is a fact attested to in the lives of AA people, who know all too well what the effort costs in the struggle through depressions and anguished doubts as they step along into recovery.

AA stories emphatically tell this message to fellow alcoholics, not as a professional prescription, not in a learned lecture, but as a style of life. Their advice to the alcoholic, after he or she has tired of social drinking as a remedy for their ills, is to see plainly what the disease of alcoholism really means, and that recovery cannot be real without stopping "their poison." It is paramount, not in the vague future, but now to take positive action, when one is sick and tired of being "sick and tired" as a drunk. The alcoholic must be forcefully confronted with this fact.

The sober majority, even family and friends, are no substitute for the down-to-earth self discovery, available from AA people in motivating and maintaining life-style sobriety. It is a life message told in the most real of reality therapies, by people who have lived through drug addiction and have kicked the habit.

Anyone knowledgeable of the alcohol addict knows that withdrawal from alcohol use is only the start of recovery. The real life problem is to motivate and maintain total sobriety. Use of supportive drugs prescribed by a knowledgeable physician is useful in some cases, but they only reach the surface of the problem. AA people know from experience how the alcoholic has a peculiar way of acquiring new drug addictions — a modification for the addictive personality. Many alcoholics today in their explorations of self-medication experiment with sedatives, downers such as barbiturates to relieve alcoholic insomnia, or amphetamines to help speed up their alcoholic depressed day. These only intensify their addiction. AA stresses recovery by recovering the inner self rather than covering the outer self with new chemical wrappings.

The Ethical Dimension

Are we saying that there is a special ethical dimension to recovery? But how can this be true in the concept of alcoholism as a disease and not a vice? Is it so startling to conceive alcoholism as bad physically and ethically? What is so special about alcoholism is the prolonged counseling required to convince the alcoholic to an honest admission of his or her disease, that to recover in health of body and spirit, there must be a change of life perspective, learning new habits of conduct, new values. This involves far more than bodily recovery, more than an external social rehabilitation. It demands personal ethical reformation.

Professionals can tell the alcoholic how to do it. But he or she must do it in life. Recovering alcoholics created AA to aid themselves and others in life-style recovery, basically of the inward person, the person in depth. This means a change for better goals, ends, motives from what is wrong for the alcoholic to what is right. It requires a search and discovery of what is good, what ought to be done in life. What is all this but an ethical dimension in the art of recovery? Do we want to play word games?

By ethical we do not mean self-righteous or punitive moralizing as a way of recovery. It is futile to try to moralize an alcoholic into recovery by confronting him or her with the charge of being a thoroughly bad person. This sort of talk only depresses the alcoholic so that the old tranquilizer is needed for emotional anesthesia. What is necessary from the beginnings of recovery is personal understanding rather than moralizing judgments.

This chapter is entitled: "The Person Who has Alcoholism" because the alcoholic is first of all a person, a human being, a man, a woman. Recovery must be first and foremost a personal adventure. It is not just an administered technique, a theory put to practice, coldly impersonal. Every person is a precious life. There is something unique about each one of us that does not fit abstract models. No two people become alcoholic in identical ways, nor do they recover in one and the same way. This is especially true in the ethical awakening of a person to the meaningfulness of recovery as a life-style.

In AA groups there are always some fellow alcoholics that the alcoholic in recovery can relate to in sharing experiences. However, the very personal character of the ethical dimension is stressed. AA people caution the recovering alcoholic not to compare his or her alcoholism with another's in a search for a perfect one-to-one relationship. Some alcoholics will end up saying that they are not that bad, perhaps not alcoholic; or, on the other hand, they may see themselves worse than they really are. So, too, no two alcoholics bottom out, experience a crisis, in an identical way. Alcoholics have encouraged themselves to continue drinking, because they have not yet fallen into the low bottoms of others. They have still a way to go, they falsely tell themselves. Each recovery is personally unique and it is basic to the ethics of recovery to respect this fundamental truth.

V. THE MORAL MIRACLE

*Rarely have we seen a person fail who has thoroughly
followed our path. Alcoholics Anonymous.*

There is a miracle that takes place at every meeting of
Alcoholics Anonymous, the moral miracle of the recovering
alcoholics who are honestly following the program day by day.
I call it moral (not moralizing) because it involves far more than
the physical recovery of a sick alcoholic. Here is recovery of
the whole person emerging step by step into a new life-style,
from the easy "yes" to a drink in an unbalanced life, to the
enlightened "yes" to meaningful sobriety in a life worth living. I
call it miraculous, because it is an extraordinary, sensible,
divine process. A human life regains self-dignity by the help of
a Higher Power, which men commonly call God, working in
the fellowship of recovering alcoholics.

At Gut Level

The moral miracle of the AA way of life is indeed extraordinary, when one considers the life-change that is effected in
salvaging a human life from the physical, spiritual, and social
disaster of the drinking alcoholic. In AA life-style recovery, the
alcoholic becomes a new person transformed in goals and
habits of life. The change is extraordinary to all who know our
AA alcoholics for what they were, and for what they are now
in living the program.

This is a sensible fact tangibly attested to by experience at
AA tables. In the course of months and years of frequent
attendance, we experience the on-going moral miracle taking
place in ourselves and fellow members. It is difficult to
counterfeit recovery, because we are all past masters in the art
of the alcoholic's camouflage. Sincere communication is easily
recognized and it is more commonly encountered. We are
talking about a very earthy, gut-level, moral miracle in the art
of building the human; the Higher Power working through the

57

fellowship in remaking a human life from hopelessness to hope.

AA recovery is no faith healing, instant happening. The shaky beginner often backtracks in alcoholic thinking and feeling, sometimes falling prey to that first easy drink. What is important is that we learn from these setbacks the benefits of living the program honestly. This is the beginning of the steady unfolding of the sober life role of human dignity. It is a beginning heavily beset by depressions, misunderstandings on our own part, and frequently from significant others in our private and social surroundings. As we look back we come to understand what this moral miracle really is in our recovery progress against such great inward and outward difficulties.

By the aid of the Higher Power — how we fought that necessary truth! Really it was more of an inward battle, perhaps against some false image of the Higher Power, as an avenging, moralizing God, a God of wrath, preachy, almost put together in a bad nursery rhyme. Perhaps it was not against God at all but "certain unreal messengers of God," the people who never took time out to understand alcoholism as a disease, but who moralized about it as a vice of a self-inflicted bum, the Skid Row image of the alcoholic.

In the AA Steps we come to experience a mode of alcoholic recovery centered in a forgiving Higher Power of love. Our unmanageable lives can be managed by belief in and surrender to this healing Power. This is indeed the core of the program especially tailored for the insecure, suspicious, untrusting alcoholic in search of relevant understanding. Of course, this is open to much misunderstanding by those who do not experience the program in an age of widespread unbelief. We are explaining the mainspring of the AA moral miracle as it is understood by those who experience it.

The Power of the Moral Miracle

The addicted alcoholic needs Almighty Power to control the all mighty power of drinking with its complex roots in a disordered, unmanageable life. In this age of apparent enlight-enment, enshrining man as the miracle worker with the will to succeed, can we believe that millions of American alcoholics, many of whom are still highly capable and respected in their fields of endeavor, cannot recover from their illness without belief in and surrender to a Power greater than themselves? To put the matter positively in terms of evidence, it is a matter of record that many thousands who follow these steps in the AA fellowship are among the recovering from alcoholism. We are talking about the most successful therapy known in recovery.

AA success is more than the human togetherness of pooling collective experiences. Collective experience affirms the ground and source of recovery strength in a Higher Power. AA is not held together by organizational ingenuity, because it is not simply an organization. It is a fellowship united in care and concern for alcoholic recovery. Left to ourselves, we alcoholics would be left to our drink compulsions. Without the Higher Power, the program is meaningless.

The moral miracle of AA is in the total sobriety of thousands of alcoholics in communities throughout the nation. Undoubt-edly, it requires more understanding in its uniqueness, in the paradox that it is so earthy and yet so spiritual, that it is so moral and yet so unmoralizing, that it is so human and yet so godly at its very core. We are not talking about the miraculous recovery of wet brains or liver cirrhosis. We are talking about the moral miracle of motivating and maintaining sobriety in a disease with a world history of tragic failures in the past.

A Spiritual Awakening

For the alcoholic to announce that he or she is undergoing a spiritual awakening may very easily be taken as a weird form of hallucination or another development of alcoholic alibis. Perhaps this is true for many who hear about the spiritual awakening, because of private distrust of such happenings, or due to past personal distrust of the alcoholic. The fact of the matter is that AA people do experience inward awakenings in their relations to God, as they understand Him, as the core of their recovery. This is not the same as saying that Alcoholics Anonymous is a form of religion or an occult mysticism. People who attend AA open meetings sometimes go away with the impression that they have just experienced some sort of "pie in the sky" happening. Admittedly, it is curious to some to hear public gratitude to God for a new life in our times of not uncommon disbelief.

The AA program is devoid of any religious indoctrination or mystical practices. AA meetings could hardly qualify as religious services. Life stories told at the tables are certainly not mystical revelations and the language at times is far from pious chatter. AA admits and accepts the power of a loving, forgiving God, as each member understands Him, in response to the need of the alcoholic in a life powerless over alcohol. The experience of the fellowship recognizes this fact.

The moral miracle of AA is never an instant recovery as in the testimony: "I will never drink again." It is a gradual, difficult, painstaking process in life. It is not just an abstinence trip, but a reforming of a life in total sobriety that calls into action the virtues of honesty, humility, patience, courage — the whole gamut of virtues required by an integral life. As in every life there are failures and defects, because the moral miracle never means that we have achieved the perfect life. What it does mean is that an alcoholic person is in daily pursuit of the good life. There is no holier-than-thou game being played. The power of recovery is not in ourselves, but in a Power higher and greater than ourselves.

The paradox of AA is that it is so divinely human. How often at the tables we hear an alcoholic say: "Here I am an important person." There is an easy experience of godly love in this fellowship. We do understand alcoholic thinking and feeling, alcoholic loneliness, depression, and alienation. The veneer of the bossy, managerial alcoholic trying to masquerade his or her insecurity is understood. The shaky beginner is seen as a type of one's own beginnings. There is understanding, too, for the alcoholic who took "another road test," and was missing for weeks. What is all important is the understanding to *keep* trying this day to follow the steps in the courage to recover.

The ideal model of the all forgiving God is by no means a soft cushion for a too easy does it recovery. Recovery has to be spurred by a raw nerve edged option for total sobriety, or insanity, or death in this deadly disease. Especially in the beginnings of the program, the alcoholic, who for years has sought emotional euphoria in the mood changing drug of ethyl alcohol, can easily fall back in his or her old ways. AA people are not shocked and given to preachy naggings at the alcoholic who steps out of the program. He or she is reached out to in benign reinforcement. For those who want help we are ready to help them back in daily living of the AA steps. The moral miracle of the Higher Power is no guarantee against lapses, if one chooses to drink. Are lapses so unusual in other diseases?

There are some who come to the program, who expect to indulge instantly in a feast of absolutes: absolutely sober, absolutely honest, absolutely solving all problems. For a person who has been so absolutely wrecking his or her life for years, such an instant change would rival walking on water. Such expectation is a symptom of the alcoholic's omnipotence. It has nothing to do with divine omnipotence. It is part of the moral miracle of AA that such omnipotent people can be calmed down to walk the earth again day by day in sober thinking, feeling, living. For people who are constitutionally capable of being honest with themselves it can be rightly said in the words of AA's *Alcoholics Anonymous* "Rarely have we seen a person fail who has thoroughly followed our path." This does not just happen by exposure to AA. It must be a Higher Power drive to action in each twenty-four hours, day by day.

A New Life-Style

The inward dimension of spiritual awakening is expressed dynamically in a new life-style. This is developed by living the Twelve Steps of the program, which we will examine in future chapters. It is a way of life that unfolds in AA people out of fellowship, yet is expressed individually in our personal life-styles. It brings to light another paradox of AA: that AA stresses individuality in communal fellowship.

There is no herd culture in AA, no merging of everyone into a stereotype mold. This is not the same as saying that some people in the program do not indulge in the game of trying to see others as themselves. However, the program itself does not intend this. Each person remains a person: Protestant, Catholic, Jew, Humanist; Republican, Democrat, Socialist; lawyer, salesman, hardhat, secretary, housewife. The common bond is in the art of living a sobriety of enduring quality in the pursuit of a meaningful life. People of diverse backgrounds, stations in life, are ardently united and easily related to one another in living recovery from the disease of alcoholism.

AA membership means more than just membership in a sort of fellowship to fill an evening or satisfy some social need. It is a vital personal response to a vital personal need. For AA to have real meaningfulness it must envelop a life with its recovery message, because its goal is to arrest a life enveloping disease, a disease that strikes at the total person. How common it is in AA to hear it said: "AA saved my life." "AA is my way of recovering." One may paraphrase it in a variety of ways. We are not just talking about an organization. We are talking about a new way of life that rids us of the old ways of the drinking alcoholic amidst a complex of attendant ills.

This new life-style is not built around the identity "alcoholic." It is centered on the human person, who has the disease of alcoholism that needs the life long vigilance of arresting. For the general public this new life-style is anonymous. AA people are not broadcasted types of a new life. Their identity is their own affair, known to God, to the fellowship, and to people they choose to share their identity with. The value of anonymity was realized at the beginnings of AA's success in recovery. The medium for spreading the AA message is deeply interpersonal among those people who have need for it, and who want it. What is more, it would be sheer nonsense for AA members to advertise themselves as winners in recovery, which by AA admission is a humble gift of the Higher Power. We did not achieve the sober life. It was given to us.

Our life-style is called new, because we change our life role from the role of the drinking alcoholic to the person in recovery. This involves, according to individual needs, a change in perspective, in behavior, in manners, in values, in goals, in friendships, in a way of life suitable to recovery. We acquire new friends in the AA fellowship. Necessarily old friends, many of whom may have been our drinking companions, are not to be dropped because of our new life-style. Rather it means a new assessment of friendship to support our vital sobriety. Strikingly it targets new ways of relaxing. Our social life and AA meetings have a special significance in this category. Our past happy hours are in dire need of substitution. It is by no accident that the cheerful and entertaining atmosphere of AA meetings and social gatherings of AA people are modifications of the jolly power we once mistakingly sought in what was really a drinking bout. This moral miracle can never really be a sad experience.

Frequent attendance at AA meetings is a must for recovery. The number of meetings should be decided upon prudently according to one's personal needs. Meetings are basic to the cultivation of a new life-style for the recovering alcoholic. AA makes no demands concerning attendance. This is a personal matter. The AA life-style of recovery comes to a person at the meetings and it is worked out in one's own way of life. The real test of this mode of living is the action of remaining in total sobriety in a meaningful life, a life worth living to ourselves and those around us. It is a gradual development arising from and continuing in spiritual inward awakening to our own human dignity with others in the world.

The self of the alcoholic enclosed in resentments, self-pity, helplessness, alienation, and dishonesty must first of all be awakened to self-identity, and with the help of fellow alcoholics in recovery corrected by positive thinking and living. Every drinking alcoholic more or less experiences this need. It is the moral miracle of AA that it answers this need in the action of doing for others who want help. Most of us as we start recovery are not aware of what an AA new life-style really means. It does not come to us in a structured blueprint, but in the spontaneity and practicality of living this program of on-going recovery of the human.

The new life of recovery begins for us when we admit and accept in the First AA Step: I am an alcoholic. I am powerless over alcohol. My life is unmanageable. This is in essence a personal identity step, identifying the problem, which in the throes of the disease we denied for so long — dodging it, alibing it, conning our way away from it. This is the beginning of the end of the identity-crisis, which is the trapgate for so many, who never do anything about their disease. Our moral miracle has begun.

VI. THE SOBRIETY GOAL

It has been said of AA, that we are interested only in alcoholism. That is not true. We have to get over drinking in order to stay alive. But anyone who understands . . . knows that no true alky ever stops drinking permanently without undergoing a profound personality change. Bill Wilson, Letter, 1940.

In these words, the co-founder of AA sums up a good description of the goal of genuine recovery. The sobriety that puts a stop to the complex disease of alcoholism is more than a dry, stop-drinking recovery. No one can gainsay the importance of abstinence from alcoholic beverages in the life of the recovering alcoholic, who is successfully following the program of AA. However, the total disease of alcoholism causing psychological, physical, and social disabilities demands a sobriety that heals the whole person. There can be no doubt that AA usage of the word "sobriety" has a special significance in the living art of alcoholic recovery.

The dictionary listings of common usages of the word "sobriety" signifying "temperance, moderation, seriousness, solemnity, gravity" do not precisely convey the meaning that AA people experience in striving for the achievement of their sobriety goal. What gives special significance to the word is not only what the AA recovering alcoholic is experiencing as he or she is wrestling with the physical, psychological, and ethical battle in moving out of the addiction, but the thinking and feeling of the drinking years. This might be called the negative side of getting sober, and especially at the start it is heavily physical. There is also the positive side of sobriety in the blessings of health, morale, self-dignity, social recognition, and spiritual serenity that come to play the larger more significant role in the sobriety goal.

Not Just Dry Sobriety — Self-Pity

What most drinking alcoholics fear in turning to recovery is the physical fear of stopping their drinking, the agonies of withdrawal, the dark depressions, the outer and inner shakes, the flaky intention of sobriety of the past. In a word, they fear a "dry sobriety," which has a special meaning for the drinking alcoholic who wants recovery to good health but fears the price he or she has to pay in painstaking effort, especially in the first stages of recovery.

Now it is part of the moral miracle of AA people that they not only quickly spot these fears but also they are able to communicate spontaneously that AA sobriety is not really a dried out affair, a solemnly serious sobriety, a fun drained life, a lock step programming from "the life of the party" to coffee drinking addicts meeting in dull basements of churches every night of the week. The AA Steps are steps from the alienation, the boredom, the misery of the drinking alcoholic to the human togetherness, the joys, and manifold goodness of building the human in the recovery of the whole person in life.

The fears of "dry sobriety" are spawned by the demon of self-pity. This is the self-pity that the drinking alcoholic feeds on inwardly and outwardly in supporting his or her drinking life. "I couldn't really make it without a drink." "You don't understand my condition. You never try to." Actually, the newcomer who wants in on recovery cannot talk this way to the AA member. They uncover what is really being said, the camouflage of self-pity to avoid a real try at honest sobriety, the fear of being honest, the fear of being helped, understood, loved. AA people have themselves been through these fears. They can communicate to their fellow alcoholics that recovery is not all negative, painful, and that the positive blessings of sobriety are what really turn us on.

Maintaining Total Sobriety

How often we hear recovering alcoholics reminisce: "Whew! I never thought I could pass that thin line of consent even to try for total sobriety — a drink-free style of living." And yet those who really want it, think it, and feel it, do cross that line and maintain a daily effort to stay across by not starting to drink again. We need help from the power of the Alcoholics Anonymous fellowship and the Higher Power to reach out in the action of recovery. AA was founded for this goal: to motivate and maintain total sobriety, free from the seriousness of a prohibitionist's exhibition of "thou shalt nots," to a happy seriousness for the positive drive to a healthy, productive life. This message comes alive in the AA meetings forcefully in the dynamics of living example: the former drunks now living weeks, months, years, decades of sobriety. There is no medicine that can be the magic bullet to give this message, no electric shock treatment, no wise analyst, no pleadings of loved ones. It comes to us by people who have gone *our way* and are going our way in recovery. Here is life-style communication not in the controlled atmosphere of a sanatorium, but in daily living by *being* in it, not just talking or listening, but in action. As some men put it: "I was socked in the gut and I wasn't quite sure what was happening to me. But I was changing into a sober being."

Alcohol is mentioned only once in the AA Twelve Steps. The sobriety game is really far more than just sobering up a drunk. It is sobering up the person in the fast game of wanting — what we want, when we want it, how we want it. It is the slow requiem of the child in us and the awakening and maintaining of the responsible adult in real interpersonal behavior. It is gaining and maintaining emotional sobriety, something that we somehow missed in our former life history.

Sobriety— Action in Living

All addicts have to get clean and stay clean from their particular kind of poison and the overdoses of poisonous thinking and emotions that fester in their personal life. This requires more than just knowing what to do, more than just wanting to do it. It means stepping into action, no zoom trip, but a gradual, serious, meaningful stepping into the long route of recovery. Easy does it, but there must be understanding and motivation that this is a rough trip, with relapses for many of us, and feelings that we won't make it at times. We need encouragement, a positive goal-directed route, with the raw courage to keep at it.

No one is really too dumb to follow the AA Steps, but there are some who consider themselves too intelligent to stay with them. This is a simple program for complex people. But sometimes our complexity turns us off. We find the AA talk trite perhaps, maybe too direct and honest. We are used to double-talk, and how we fear exposure of our con games. We like to procrastinate, to drink a little perhaps and try a little to get sober. AA hits us at center. "You have to get honest. Realize that to drink means to get drunk. See your problem not mainly in others but in yourself. Get with the action of self-correction. To hell with self-pity. Start helping yourself. Give yourself a clean break. The time is now."

How the sensitivities of the drinking alcoholic exposed to AA for the first time are shocked by the plain talk! Especially the educated, sophisticated drunk who tries to get analytical and break up the direct attack on his or her boozing. There are long monologues on the theories of alcoholism and somehow the alcoholic is lost in the theorizing. AA points out that we have to keep it simple. Get into the action of stopping the poisoning of the alcoholic's life, the action of simply guarding oneself at gut level to stop the drinking. Get a clear head and a manageable life this day. No drinking alcoholic can really take any one of the AA Steps. How that message socks it to us. We scream inside and some just won't face this basic to any real recovery. Isn't there a pill to do it for us? Really, did anyone ever get sober in playing the abstract game: "Why do I drink, when it is ruining my life?"

AA has no official theory of alcoholism. It has Twelve Steps for doing recovery that work for many thousands who are constitutionally capable of being honest enough to get into the action and maintain it as a life-style. We are talking about practical knowledge, action for crisis — and the alcoholic actively in the lethal disease of alcoholism *is* in a crisis. AA endeavors to get through to the person activating his or her disease in an effort to arrest it, to control it not by substitutes of other chemical dependency. The message is, the action of substituting a recovery life-style, substituting recovery thinking and feeling, constructive friendships, occupation and recreation, for the old habits of living built around a glass crutch, a bottled-in cage. This is no self-hypnosis of group-addicts, but a personal awakening in the action of doing what is necessary to live and enjoy! There is no sudden miracle here like walking on water, but the miracle of the ordinary. The person who wanted to trip out in the clouds comes down to earth.

No Holier-Than-Thou Sobriety

Authentic sobriety never emerges in a spiritually proud person, as one steps into a real personality transformation. We realize that we are not doing the program of recovery alone. We owe it to our Higher Power of forgiving love and to the godly people of AA. We are humbled in this self-revelation. No one really recovers without recovery in the humble prayer of on-going gratitude. There is always the danger that we may start comparing ourselves to Mr. Clean, Mrs. Clean, Miss Clean, and those poor drunks who just won't make it. Real understanding of the alcoholic in recovery must be an understanding of humility. We are humbled in the fact that someone as damaged as we are can be as restored as we are and all of this by the free gift of love working through a humble anonymous fellowship.

The founders of AA, Bill and Dr. Bob, discovered at the beginning that alcoholics do not successfully approach the Higher Power as other people do. Particularly, alcoholics have to be careful of a leap into the spiritual. It can become another ego trip and sort of holier-than-thou syndrome. The co-founders had been in Dr. Buchman's Oxford Groups and learned many important spiritual insights there. However,

UNDERSTANDING THE RECOVERING ALCOHOLIC

alcoholics require a special spiritual program, not overly spiritual, or lofty in tone and emphasis. In the Chapter on the Higher Power, we shall return to this theme.

In our recovery toward a maintained total sobriety of the whole person, we must understand that we are undergoing a daily and steady inner growth that has special dangers for alcoholics. Drinking alcoholics are cursed with false pride, and are closed in persons, who are not really aware of what is happening in depth. As we emerge we cannot afford to let this pride modify itself into believing that we are special people of the Lord, free from all fears, all problems, thoroughly serene. We are still very much a part of the human scene.

In a sense we are the winners, as we stay with the program day by day, but we are not winners, who did it our own way, alone, by our own power. The knights of the round table are alive and well, while the sick world wallows around us. We all still bear the marks of that sickness within us. In fact, for our kind of illness, it is only an arm's length away to explode in our lives. New members in the honeymoon of their newly experienced sobriety have to listen well to the understanding of veteran AA's, who know only too well what spiritual pride can do to alcoholics in recovery.

The first taste of sobriety, the novel experience of knowing that we can say "no" to a drink, quiet resentments, live with depressions of our withdrawal, can urge us to proclaim this moral miracle to the world and even denounce our drinking buddies or sisters, who won't dry out with us. We are, in our own eyes in this emotional honeymoon, giants of a new cause. Actually we are in fragile infantile steps of the program. Thank God for the knowledgeable AA's around us, who can tell us that this roar of the lion is really the squeak of a mouse. (Of course, there are ways of breaking it to us more gently.) Our high emotional bliss can be a signal of imagined security to leave us unprepared for the emotional blues and blahs. The shock of descent can lead to a blast with the glass.

In the AA experience, humility is always the name of the game. Veteran members can also be subject to this spiritual pride we have been describing in different moods and modes. They can fall into the notion that they are unshakeable in the AA Steps and discover anew how insidious the disease can be. This can be brought home to an AA after many years of sobriety in times of success or sorrow. No one of us is totally immune to drinking again and setting off again the dreaded progress of the disease. No one has finished complete sobriety until his or her life is complete. Finished sobriety can only be proclaimed in a eulogy. To live the program means that we live a risk. But after all, isn't this what life is all about?

"Can I Get Sober?"

This chapter would go badly unfinished without a word to the reader in need of the sobriety message but still crippled by the thought: "Man, how I need it, but I can't just get it." In AA the "I can't" is changed into the "We can." We can do it as others have done it and are doing it by the moral miracle of the Higher Power coming our way in the very earthy circumstances of a godly fellowship of recovery understanding in action. Undoubtedly, no book can cover all the possible emotional blocks that prevent a life from trying for sobriety with success day by day. The living action of AA, however, has its own way of getting through. Try it. Maybe you won't like it at first. But it is worth the try and the chances are in your favor that in some way you will have gained by honestly trying.

There is no disease quite like the special drug addition of alcoholism. Radically, the problem of recovery is not simply drug withdrawal. The problem is people: the alcoholic in need of understanding himself and being understood by others. AA is a people's response, people who are actively addicted, who come to be motivated and maintain a life-style sobriety of enduring quality. The addict with a needle is easily spotted. The alcohol addict with a glass may hide for a time in the crowd or in his privacy. He or she may not know what is happening to him or her, as many of us can recollect, but when the disease hits, when it really hits, it explodes a life. It is

71

just too big to put the scramble together on one's own. Perhaps the reader knows well what I am talking about. Sobriety that is total is far more than a man powered event. It is a gift of life of all the living, as we come to understand life.

Bill W., AA's co-founder, stresses the fact that the spiritual aspect is the first to go in alcoholic progression and it can go very subtly. It goes with self dishonesty. The question, "Can I get sober?" must be understood as the self questioning: "Can I really get honest with myself?" Truly, the first step in spiritual awakening is the down-to-earth self honesty step — to be really real with oneself. This brings us to admission and acceptance in Step One of the AA program.

VII. ADMISSION AND ACCEPTANCE

Step One: We admitted that we were powerless over
alcohol, that our lives had become unmanageable.

For the recovering alcoholic, never was so much said in so
few words. In terms of the past, our admission sums up a
miasma of misery, for the present it signifies a victory in defeat,
and for the future the hope of recovering human dignity. We
are speaking here about the first step in our recovery, and not
a return to the first step in the continuing living of the AA
program. For indeed there is no return to the first step that can
relive the experience of the beginner, the man or woman who
begins recovery by admission of defeat of the drinking
alcoholic, and the hope of recovery through the victory of a
sobriety of ethical quality. In Step One we admit our defeat by
drinking in our powerlessness and the unmanageability of our
lives. It is a cry for help from the abyss, out of the depths of our
bottoming out. And yet there is victory in this defeat. We have
the power to seek help and through our fellowship to manage
the starting of our admission of hope through recovery.

We speak of the victory of admission. At last we see
ourselves as we are and we admit it. We want recovery,
although we are not sure what all this entails. What we do
know in AA admission is that the way of recovery is to sobriety
through total abstinence. In our admission we are open to
learn how to step into this way by a new style of living. This is
for us the important step of our lives, because up to now there
was in us no real drive to recover, only the drinking life. This is
the ethical victory of admission, and the dawning of the moral
miracle of recovery in our lives.

We have emerged from the emotionally immature, selfish,
fantasyland of the drunk, who took recovery lightly or not at
all. The wonderland of a hallucinating brain has come down to
earth to exposure for what it is, a wild escape, which was really
no escape. We were in fact the prisoner of one of the most

73

deadly sicknesses known to man. Admission can be made best when we are hurting the most. There is no time for rationalizing our condition, for disguising it. It is there in all its agony, the wet hell of the drunk.

AA admission is especially open to misunderstanding, by the sober majority. For people who do not know the dark experience of the addicted alcoholic, who are accustomed to lengthy, calm deliberation before decision, who have the luxury of deciding for themselves rather than to be moved by circumstance to decision, for these people understanding alcoholic admission under the stress and strain of catastrophe can very well be taken as an admission of sheer emotionalism. Somehow a purging of life by an emotional change from the bad to the good has escaped them. Experts sometimes tell us that alcoholics are in special need of emotional change because of their sensitive natures. And the experts themselves are very sensitive to any criticism of this theory.

Is it not true that this is the story of human life, a passionate engagement in our style of sensitive living? The alcoholic is but one example of this passion for living. A positive admission is a kind of admission of futility in a bad life-choice that many people would like to make, but do not quite know how to go about it. The honesty of AA admission is indeed paradoxical. The more we ponder the plight of the human, the less exceptional the alcoholic really appears, and the more we come to an understanding of the real human quality of AA admission. But to admit and accept this honestly, amidst our ground-swell of human phoniness, is a kind of moral miracle!

It Hurts

Admission can be made best when the alcoholic is really hurting. This requires explanation. It certainly does not mean that a delirium tremens would be the ideal time for strong alcoholic admission. We are speaking here of the total awareness that a person experiences of bodily and spiritual helplessness over alcohol, the unmanageability of life due to drinking. Such a person knows that he or she cannot live as a human being with this condition, and seeks help. They realize they cannot do it alone. This admission of recovery so commonly experienced in AA is the first step of recovery. It is strongly negative to the alcoholic life and the start of the positive search for recovery. There is great fear of the disease experienced, mingled with an almost instinctive hope in life. It is nonsense to say that all man has to fear is fear itself. Fear, as indeed every emotion, has a good role to play in the changing scene of life.

Step One begins where the action is, the drinking alcoholic, knowledgeable enough now to know what alcoholism is in personal life. It is the admission of a defeated person as an active alcoholic but not the defeat of a person as a person. The punishments of drinking have come to far outweigh any gratifying rewards. It is the first step in the defeat of the drinking alcoholic, and the beginning of personal hope in recovery.

Do we see now why AA begins with the cry from the depths, why we do not begin with lofty motivations such as love of wife, family, good name, successful living? We begin where we are. Every drinking alcoholic progressing into or in the disease is a person in real distress. The main distress is himself or herself. The main torment is self-torment. It is strangely our torment of indecision of living a hell, and in some weird way wanting hell, as if it has become a precious part of us. The experience still waits verbal formulation. It may never be told. Self-understanding is rarely a case of telling. It is more personal than commonly verbal. It is surrender at a non-verbal, primitive level.

In every admission the heart and core of admission is never spoken. If it is real, it is lived at the start in horror and hope, the horror of the alcoholic self refusing to die, to go away; the hope of the recovering self to break through and take over. Authentic admission is the requiem of the drink drive of our life. It is a continuing process that lives on in all steps of recovery. Reflective admission begins as a kind of dialogue going on in the struggle of Step One between phases of the ego. How unreal is the impression that admission is an instant miracle, a timed verbal statement once made, and then on we go happily to Step Two, and probably back to the bar and "I'll drink to that."

Victory in Defeat

Victory in defeat — this is the genuine thrust of admission. But what really is the defeat and what is the victory? Certainly it is not the final victory of sobriety. We never complete the way of recovery in the First Step, although some of us take it in the big stride of a jolly green giant, green in our newness to any sobriety. Our defeat is really the start of the death of the lie that we have been living, the lie of false identity, the inability to face ourselves as a sick people, powerless and unmanageable. We liked to believe that alcohol was our power, that it was our life, relief from the squirrel cage of our existence.

In admission we come to our first victory in recovery, which is to be our daily victory in the admission, "I am an alcoholic, powerless over alcohol. It is my defeat. I must not drink." This admission needs the prudence of veteran, fellow recovering alcoholics to guide us, so that it becomes for us a healing admission, rather than an admission that makes our lives more unmanageable. How pitiable is the dried out alcoholic with no morale, no spirit. He is ready for another try at the number one tranquilizer.

This is no bar room admission, no hangover swan song, no uncountable replay of the broken record of our alcoholic promises. It must be made soberly in reflection, within the fellowship at the First Step table in a conditioned atmosphere of understanding and counsel. There we are made keenly aware of what we are admitting through frequent attendance at meetings. To understand the drinking alcoholic is to understand a person with an identity crisis. In Step One we are beginning to understand our disease, but there is a deeper personal awakening.

76

We are at the dawning of understanding ourselves in honesty and humility. It is a shock experience, because we are not used to taking an honest and humble look at ourselves. We are learning new habits, a new life perspective. It is more than a case of knowledge. It is a case of learning by doing. It is a difficult step like the first step of an infant, because we are stepping out of our infantile self, the self that refused to mature emotionally for so many years. We may be even secretly crying now like an infant for "the bottle."

Generally, sick people respond eagerly to the danger signals of their illness. Alcoholics too frequently wait until the danger signals explode in technicolor. In most diseases the sick fear the consequences of their illness and seek medical help. In so many cases the alcoholic is literally carried in for treatment. We had to fight the common cry of the alcoholic: "I am not an alcoholic." It takes a crisis awakening education to make us respond. Alcoholics are prone to wait until their crisis brings a doctor to their bedside, or brings them to a hospital, to learn their sick identity. Even then admission may be timed up to the date of their hospital recovery, or when the doctor tells them they have recovered from the bout.

It is a gross misunderstanding to assume that drinking alcoholics do not know they are sick people in the progression of their disease. Pain in the body, anguish of spirit, social disaster, actual or threatening, are not goodies of the healthy. What is curious about alcoholics is that they will not meaningfully admit their illness. We all know how we delayed action, how we procrastinated, until we were awakened by some sort of bottoming out, in some cases acute and cruel, in others more threatening, and realized in bitter perspective of worse things to come. There is no one overall picture of a crisis awakening. In fact even the recovering alcoholic cannot decode it in detail on serious examination. What is a real awakening for one, is easily passed over by another.

Drinking alcoholics are living enigmas of man's claim to being a rational animal, notwithstanding our not uncommon possession of high IQ's and responsible positions. We insanely

77

follow a way of gradual suicide by camouflaging it through innumerable clever ploys of self-disguise. It is more than a case of hiding bottles, sneaking drinks. It is the role of disguise of what one really is from oneself, the self-torment of living a hell, and believing it to be a tranquilizer. This is part of the drug dependency disease. All of this the recovering alcoholic is fighting in his or her continuing admission in the First Step. These first days and weeks and even months of admission are a real battleground. They can mean for us the victory of recovery admission, that our defeat is in active alcoholism. We are admitting help into our lives.

Half Measures Avail Us Nothing

No drinking alcoholic is just somewhat attracted to alcohol. It is never a case of half measured craving. It is an all out affair. So, too, no recovering alcoholic recovers by half measures or a half-hearted, casual effort. Recovery has to begin and continue in a simple, all-out heroic commitment of admission in life to total sobriety. One drink spoils the scene. Half measures avail us nothing.

This basic truth is paramount to understanding the recovering alcoholic. It is the gut-level discovery of the AA fellowship and a fundamental step in why AA works. A drinking alcoholic is not recovering. One drink is too much for the addicted. It is the initial step to activating the disease, the mainspring in the chain reaction of the alcoholic's drinking. Alcohol is the chemical trigger of alcoholism.

Self-evident, you say? Even easy to admit in the honeymoon of recovery — but will this vigilance last? The record attests that many alcoholics become victims again of this insidious disease. Our AA groups also attest that many do maintain total sobriety by living the AA steps. The program is slip proof. The root of AA vigilance is activating the choice for sobriety, not thinking that first drink, not allowing rationalizations for drinking to take over; by putting them down at the very start.

This disease never has a quiet requiem as recovery breaks through in our lives. How often we hear it said at First Step tables: "I have a disease that wants to tell me that I don't have a disease." Our new experience of recovery can be a real danger zone. Half measures are getting to us when we begin to confuse our powerlessness over alcohol with the power of recovery; when we feel that we are well enough to drink to that! Our loss of control over alcohol can be confused with our regained control in a manageable life so that we think that we can manage a drink without going back to our addicted drinking. And so we have to learn again the insidiousness of this disease.

AA experience testifies that recovery is not something to be taken for granted in times when things are going well, but also in times of stress and fatigue. This, however, does not mean that recovery is to be lived out in fear and trembling of failure. The recovering have to believe in themselves, in a healthy spirit of self-esteem and self-worth, to choose what is right.

Genuine Admission Never Self Excuse

Now at last we are learning to tell it as it is in recovery. We are discarding the ridiculous masquerade more really tragic than comic in the style of W.C. Fields' act of the humorous drunk. Our masquerade was usually verbalized in various self-declared "motives" for heavy drinking. Some of us said we drank to spur us on in the pressure of work. Others drank because they could not work at all without it. Some drank to escape their dull, incomplete existence. Still others blamed it on their swinging society, their way of Falstaffian life as a high pressure salesman. A worker puts the blame on the dull assembly line. Rare indeed is the admission of the truth: "I drink because I am a sick alcoholic. I drink out of an addiction." How true is the raw reality that alcoholics do not just drink. They feed a sickness, an addiction. The alcohol addict does not drink a beverage. He or she is addicted to a drug. The alcoholic's drinking is always different with a sickening difference. His or her glass is a glass crutch.

Is this an excuse to shift the blame from our moral selves to our sick selves? Many of the sober majority, who are used to excuses from us, when they hear our admission that we are powerless over alcohol, that our lives are unmanageable in drinking, hear a different story than we intend. Some cannot believe that we are admitting to recovery. They are so used to our disguises that they may easily take this as a new excuse for drinking — out of a disease. After all, we are powerless and the power of drink can turn us on, would you believe, only an arm's length away. We must expect misunderstanding, and this is why the fellowship of understanding is so necessary in a life-style of sobriety. This is why daily attendance at our AA group is important to our First Step recovery beginnings. Our spouse and family must realize this.

It is a popular belief that alcoholics morally choose their condition. They are alcoholics because of a vice. Excessive drinking is self-inflicted. There is some important truth in this approach. Morality does enter the scene as a main theme, but it is not the whole story basically. No one having the vices of lying, false pride, resentfulness, or despondency turns up with an alcoholic's diseased body. It takes a peculiar type of body chemistry, those peculiar X factors, to become an addicted alcoholic in the disease of alcoholism. Of course, our immorality helped as a partial mainspring and with good medicine and proper psychological aid, morality is the mainspring in arresting the disease in a life-style choice of admission to total sobriety.

When we begin to understand all that is said here, we begin to understand the moral program of AA. It is no instant hallelujah to sobriety. On the physical side you may catch a cold, but you do not "catch" alcoholism. You are *potentially* alcoholic, as a particular kind of human, and you only know it by drinking. It is no sudden discovery, just as personal recovery to sobriety and better living is not sudden, but through a continuing admission of what we are and what we hope to be.

Joys of Admission

The nitty gritty facts of admission must be told, but this does not mean that admission is only a calvary of agony. Humanly we could only stay with it because of its many joys. There is the experience of conquest. We can abstain and, what is more, we can abstain because we can feel that we do not need to drink. There is more to life. There is the joy of sober reconciliation with our family, our friends, our efficiency on the job. There is the discovery of the human in us, the value of humility, honesty, patience, and real love. Can we describe the simple bodily joys of waking up fresh and lively in the morning, greeting another day without hang-over pains, without the fear of falling apart! Continuing admission is enlivened by the daily simple rewards of sobriety, which others take so easily for granted. There is a special sensitivity to the ordinary goods of living.

Every alcoholic in recovery is admitting to a defeat in his or her drinking career — defeat of an alcoholic psychoneurosis, the personality with a long list of bad traits, to defeats of bodily sickness, especially in one's physical loss of control in drinking, to defeats of social failures; but we are also admitting to the joyous victory of self-discovery and actualization. We can say: "I have come this far. I have another day of sobriety. I can change. I have seen it in veteran AA members with many years of sobriety with histories of hard drinking like my own."

There is a negative and a positive aspect to every admission. Admission is not merely negative by admitting to powerlessness and unmanageability, because we make the admission for the sake of regaining power and manageability in our affairs. No alcoholic's admission ever led to recovery by negations, prohibitions, mere abstinence. One can abstain in a way that means abdication from the joy of living. This was our fear of recovery in our drinking days. Alcoholics recover by accen-

81

tuating the positive in the joy of living. AA has really brought a new meaning to sobriety beyond just being abstemious, temperate, grave, sedate, not intoxicated. AA sobriety aims at being comfortably in self-control, the reasonably human life. The fellowship educates us to think positively.

The Negative and the Positive

Every admission is strongly negative to drink, especially the first drink that sets off the chain reaction sooner or later in loss of control. Admission is born out of the dregs of alcoholism. But it does not stay there. It develops in a lively "yes" to the sanity and health of sobriety, the living of the good life in all of one's affairs. This is the positive spring of admission, the hope of recovery. It is admission to a hopeful change of habits, a learning of a new style of living, a new perspective, new goals.

There is no mere going back to our good lives before we drank. We have the drinking problem, the disease has been activated. In recovery we do not just return to our former lives. Really we have to remake our lives. It is a brand new challenge. Some do not fully realize this. They act like cured patients, ready to begin where they left off before their heavy drinking catastrophe. This is not reality for us. Recovery is a life-style to arrest a disease that has been strongly activated. Our addiction is not cured. We must learn to live with it in a normal and productive manner. "But how does one go about it?" This is the question.

Every beginner has times of doubts in his or her admission. These have a way of arising at the most unsuspected moments, in times of success in sobriety, in times of good health and buoyancy of spirit, when things are going our way. The thought surfaces: "Maybe I am not alcoholic after all, not addicted. Maybe it was just a passing event." Truly the problems of our drinking days may be passing away, but the problem of drinking is in us in a disease form. It is there as a prepared potency ready to surprise us. And how it does, when we experiment with social drinking!

82

Maybe we drink socially for an evening, maybe for some weeks, maybe on occasion for a few months, but then inebriation happens and this time with more strength than before. It is as if our bodies are yelling at us, "Dummy, wake up, we are still all together, the alcoholic's body and the supposedly tempered spirit of the social drinker." Have we forgotten so easily this dialogue featuring Jekyll and Hyde, that we have played so often in the past?

Test Questions and that First AA Meeting

AA begins with heavy focus on alcoholic drinking, the obvious problem. Every alcoholic does some damage to his or her life and to the lives of others by drinking. The common American variety of alcoholics with the disease of addiction have their own special damage set off by drinking. AA tries to make the alcoholic aware of what it means to say: "I am powerless over alcohol, my life is unmanageable when I drink." The beginner is given a list of test questions to review in coming to his or her decisive admission: "I am an alcoholic." We list some of the more salient questions here.

Commonly, this is one examination that we pass with large percentages. Maybe we cannot answer "yes" to every question, but we can see the "yes" coming. It is not for freshmen in the career of drinking. These questions are to be read slowly with reflection on one's life before answering.

Has drinking changed your personality?

Is your drinking harming your family in any way?

Does drinking cause you bodily complaints?

Has your efficiency decreased since drinking?

Is drinking jeopardizing your business?

Have you less self-control since drinking?

Do you drink to relieve marked feelings of inadequacy?

Has drinking made you irritable?

Do you have the inner shakes unless you continue drinking?

Do you prefer to drink alone?

Does drinking cause you to have difficulty in sleeping?

Do you require a drink the next morning?

Has drinking made you more impulsive?
Do you show marked dislikes and hatreds since drinking?
Is drinking clouding your reputation?
Is drinking affecting your peace of mind?
Is drinking disturbing your harmony of life?

These questions are not needed by the usual beginners in AA to know about the damage of drinking for them. They bring their answers more or less subconsciously with them into AA. They are part of their life stories. The test questions are given only to impress in bold detail the conscious meaning of alcoholism in one's life. A careful reading of the work entitled *Alcoholics Anonymous,* co-authored by Bill and Dr. Bob, founders of AA, is important as an introduction to the meaning of AA admission and its continuing process in AA recovery. Of course, studied reflection is generally difficult for many in the beginning. Talking difficulties out with fellow AA members over coffee, in private informal meetings, over the telephone, these are valuable aids in coming to terms with admission. There is far more implied in admission than we ordinarily suppose. It is not uncommon that beginners misunderstand it as a timed event, that happens when we first come to AA, a first step once taken, and then passed on.

Actually we grow in our personal admission as we grow in recovery. We come to realize how very much is involved in saying "no" to a first drink, and a lively "yes" to a meaningful sobriety of life. It is a continuing life-style of on-going rewards that we do not want to leave off. It becomes a part of our life. This is why veteran AA members are happy to sit in at First Step tables. Each day in our lives is really a new First Step in admission. We are not just admitting a no-drinking life, we are filling life with the true, the good, and the beautiful. And this is no put-on. This is the moral miracle of recovering alcoholics, not ex-alcoholics, who have found a new philosophy of life amidst the devaluing of all values in our times.

From the very start the beginner is not only experiencing the blues and blahs of admission, but also its rewards in recovery. Inner fears and social difficulties do not just disappear, but we

84

learn to live with them gradually in a fellowship of understanding and counsel. Our first meeting always has its special fear as we face the group. We do not know them. What will it be like? Will we see someone we know, who will discover that we are alcoholic? We forget we are meeting with fellow alcoholics who prize their own anonymity.

From the beginning we sense a new experience of belonging, an important step out of our alienation, our inner loneliness. There is in us a growing desire to relate, to release long pent up misunderstandings. This being at home in AA develops more quickly in some of us. Quite often we begin with a certain hesitancy, but always with some comfort of knowing there is an alcoholic fellowship, a place of comradeship, a program of recovery, that we come to see profoundly working in lives similar to our own. Powerless, unmanageable lives of drinkers are changed into recovered power of control and manageability. "Right on," we say. "It is worth our effort."

Acceptance

This chapter is called admission and acceptance because every admission that is genuine must be a continuing acceptance of what we are and what we hope to be. No one honestly admits alcoholic addiction and the way of recovery, and at the same time sets out to try drinking. There is an inner logic to the program of recovery, but we all have to fight the reality of a life that is not all logical, all upward and forward, all sanitized in body and spirit.

Admission, when it is honest, is an acceptance of the contest to be sober, to improve life with all its bitter-sweet compound. We must accept our frailties, deeply impressed on us by years of drinking, years of doing our own thing, years of copping out from responsibilities. This hang-up does not just disappear by good intentions. No one of us is that good. Sooner or later we will be humbled in this discovery. What is important is that we do not let the frailties take over, and when they do, to fight on to regain living our admission.

There are days when the beginner experiences emotional highs. It is easy to say "no" to a drink. There is the spontaneous feeling that we do not need it and even do not want it. We are even understanding of others, when people do not respond our way. We are patient when things do not go our way. Everything seems suffused with the joy of sobriety. We are conquering the big problem of our lives, and all else seems really unimportant. But there are days of the blues and the blahs when our sobriety is difficult, when we cannot understand why people do not respond to us, and things do not go our way.

The drinker in us wants to come alive, to seek relief in our number one tranquilizer, the sedation that numbs our troubled consciousness. There are the times when admission really begins to grow in meaningfulness, when we learn to accept our addiction, to control it, and to seek to manage ourselves in our affairs. It involves quieting our resentments, humbling ourselves. Our struggle is not just against the bad in us. It is also for the revival of the good, and to sustain the good in us. Accentuating the positive, giving a hard look at the real joys of sobriety, and the remembered misery of drinking, can sustain us.

Patience can reward us in time, and the good in us takes over. We are learning the important art of substitution. We are creating new wants, developing new goods for ourselves and service to others through sobriety. One cannot sell anything to a satisfied person. Certainly we admit and accept that we cannot be satisfied with the disaster of our loss of control in drinking. Therefore, we make ourselves want something new. We are striving to remove our active drive to drink by substituting the drive to meaningful sobriety, real joy in living. This is the hard sell to ourselves of a new life. We need a new and more durable mood changer than alcohol, and we find the answer in the AA Twelve Steps of recovery.

What if we do fall, succumb to the first drink, absurdly suppose that we are social drinkers again, believe that AA somehow has cured us, only to find ourselves sooner or later smashed in our old folly? We are left stewing in a ground swell of remorse, self-pity, the dark cellar of resentments. Some beginners indulge in the self-pity that acceptance of recovery is useless for them. They cannot accept sobriety. Many, however, recover from their failures, because they expose their weakness. They really did not want to accept the real loss of control when they did drink. They know that to stay with drinking means an unfolding of more and more powerlessness and unmanageability. They want the program, and they make a more honest and humble try at it again. They have learned from their mistakes. They have hope in the struggle to accept the AA style of living. These stories are common in AA.

VIII.   BUILDING THE HUMAN

All members of "the recovery team" must be endowed
with abundant amounts of patience, tolerance,
understanding and sincere personal interest. Dr. Karl E.
Voldeng in Recovery from Alcoholism.

AA recovery action means becoming a living part of the fellowship. The abundant amount of patience, tolerance, understanding, and sincere personal interest that we experience from our group enables us to step into the action. We are recovering when we find ourselves reaching out, sharing, and caring. Alcoholism is a lonely disease. Participation in AA group activities gradually comes to the newcomer out of the attraction to fellow recovering alcoholics.

The wall of isolation gradually comes down in the friendly spirit of the group. Doing small tasks like making coffee, sharing in setting up chairs for a meeting, pitching in to clean up after a meeting, may seem of small value but they pay big dividends in stepping out of the enclosed alcoholic's isolation. Joining in the speaker's forum, telling stories of what it was like before recovery, and what is happening now is a healing experience that surprises us in our new found initiative. The group does not expect newcomers to plunge into the action. It does take time. Especially after ninety days of meetings, which are suggested for novices, these tasks grow into an outgoing life-style of sharing and caring.

Importance of a Sponsor

In the days of hard beginnings the role of a sponsor can help to steady the troubled beginner. There is nothing formal in this role as indeed there is nothing formal about anything in AA. The person who is sponsoring us simply enters into this relationship by sharing experiences with us. We accept a sponsor as a guiding influence in our lives. Often this is the person who introduced us to AA, and to whom we looked for guidance as we stepped into admission, and began to accept the way of recovery. Sponsors are usually experienced in the Twelfth Step. They are people who particularly relate to us, sometimes in their stories of their own difficult beginnings, in their easily communicated honesty and willingness to help.

It must be remembered that recovering alcoholics have the heavy traits of years of self-protected independence, wanting and doing what they want. They have fears of intimate relations, suspicions of dependence on others, fears of hidden controls, of being manipulated. It takes some time to adjust to the easy, relaxed, and overt honesty of AA fellowship. Beginners are usually wary of some kind of soft sell, some preachy persuasion that will suddenly explode all over, and that they will be taken in, manipulated by unseen higher forces. We are so used to that kind of world at the mercy of hidden persuaders in a consumer society. It does not take a good sponsor long to convince a scared beginner that he or she is not being absorbed into a big organization, that a person is being cared for in a friendly fellowship, that there is no high force but a Higher Power, a loving God, that recovery is a personal discovery of the good life and not a manipulated program.

There are, of course, people who try to play the role of sponsor before they have properly equipped themselves in following the AA Steps. Usually, however, the fellowship acts as a corrective. Sponsors more generally develop healing friendship for the shaky beginner. It is more than a mere case of rapping together, sharing common experiences. It is an awakening to the action of AA in arresting the insidious disease by real living, passed on from an experienced member to a newly recovering alcoholic. There is more here than faith and courage in another person and this is brought home to us in time. It is all part of the moral miracle of recovery by the Higher Power, who is empowering an AA member to succeed and pass on this strength to another.

In the example of fellow members, and particularly our sponsor, we come to our first personal admission in AA. "My name is Ken; I am an alcoholic." So many thousands of people in AA groups are verbally making this admission and learning to enjoy it. The word "alcoholic" generally is a label of social opprobrium, a taboo in polite society. It has the ring of the doomsday bell. But this is not the case in the AA fellowship. It is the sound of honest identity. In the First Step the new member learns how to identify his or her problem as a step to recovery. It is a radical part of the alcoholic's disease that he labors in an identity crisis. In conquering it, we never go it alone. There is our sponsor beside us and the fellowship around us.

AA admission is a prudent admission made in the understanding fellowship of Alcoholics Anonymous. Especially at the beginning, members need the guidance of veteran members in expressing their admission outside the meetings. There are enthusiastic new members, who want to broadcast it to the world. The mouth that roared at the bar now wants to roar sobriety. We soon find our alcoholism is no big news to people who really knew us. They recognized our illness by our repeated performance.

A commonsense approach is needed in asserting our admission. It should be made to those people who ought to know that personally we now admit our alcoholism and are attempting to arrest it. It is futile just to admit it for the sake of admission. Moreover, we must expect some disbelief, some misunderstanding about our admission to hopeful recovery from people, even friends and family. They may easily remember past admissions and failures.

Al-Anon family groups were founded to help the family of the alcoholic to understand. They serve a vital role in the AA program. The distrust and impatience of a spouse uninformed of AA work can be a weakening, if not disastrous experience, for the alcoholic in his or her admission. A family uninformed in the disease-concept of alcoholism can fail by commission and omission along the difficult road of recovery. Sponsors serve a needed role in introducing the alcoholic's family to Al-Anon counseling.

Group Therapy

Group therapy in talking out our admissions and difficulties at First Step tables is important. There is a variety of moods and modes of admissions revealed in the voice of each speaker, in the life story that a man or woman tells. There is the hesitant, nervous, weak sounding voice of the beginner, the comfortable admission of the veteran, habituated to the practice after years of attendance at meetings. There is the eager admission of the member experiencing the first comforts of sobriety, and the painful admission of the experimenter, who thought that he or she could drink socially again. There is the bull blast of the bragging admission, and the aggravated admission of the person who has learned to say "no" to the first drink, but does not quite know how to say "yes" to joyful sobriety. Still, the moral miracle of admission pervades the AA meetings, and one can only appreciate this paradox by understanding what admission means to the alcoholic.

No one of us came to admission easily in the rough days of stepping into the recovery program. Serenity is not the overall name of the game. Admission is not just saying out loud to the group, "I am an alcoholic." Admission must be personally meaningful. It is not just the conclusion of a rational argument, nor an entirely joyful experience in a pleasant awakening to personal identity. It is not a calm, reflective, personal discovery. Nor is it only a mental admission verbally spoken. I can admit that I am an alcoholic, yet never make it an admission of the whole man in life; that I accept an admission of hope for a better life, not a sterile, no drinking life.

It takes us a long time to realize that sobriety is not just abstinence, but an opening up to the fullness of meaningful life. This calls for a life change, not just a change of mind. AA admission is a deliberate, mental, practical admission that I am an alcoholic, and that I have the hope for a better life. It is born in a struggle. This is the ideal AA admission that gradually grows and matures in the recovering member in the fellowship

91

living the Twelve Steps. In this context AA admission is a step that is forever unfinished, because it pervades each day of our lives. We are arresting a life-time disease. The challenge is for life.

Admission to an Insidious Disease

Admission does not come easily, because we are admitting to an insidious disease, damnably cunning. It is insidious, because it attacks the whole man, body and spirit, individually and socially. At a time when brainpower and spirit in life are most needed, when we alcoholics decide to leave our drinking alcoholism, we are found most wanting. The alcoholic disease cripples us in the very core of our being. Left to ourselves we would become part of the countless failures in the past, the all too common world history of the hopelessness of the disease. It takes a real miracle to resurrect us.

AA focuses the admission of an alcoholic as a human being on himself or herself, powerless and unmanageable, in order to spur the cry for help in fellowship with other recovering alcoholics to the Higher Power. We are not speaking here, as is plainly evident, of the cry for medical help, even psychiatric help; we are talking about help to maintain sobriety in a life-style for the recovery of the human in us, not just a repaired body or a repaired psyche. AA does not focus admission centrally on alcohol. The emphasis throughout the program is on the human person, who needs to be motivated, activated back into the human family.

AA admission of powerlessness and unmanageability is sometimes misunderstood as a totally humiliating, passive acceptance of help, as if we have nothing to do but to be helped, because we are so wrecked internally and externally by our disease. These are not our AA people who live the capacity to recover.

AA admission is made in sobriety as an admission to maintain sobriety. Sobriety means on-going control and manageability. We accept help from God and the fellowship to strengthen that control and manageability into a life program that we would otherwise be too weak to endure. We know there will be rough times, but our inner strength is reinforced by making our will strong in divine strength embodied in the fellowship. There is no weakling puppet game of being strung along by unseen hands from above. It is not a case of doing nothing, and letting the Higher Power turn us on. *We have to accept.*

It cannot be overstated that AA is not a substitute for medicine or psychiatry. There is some misunderstanding in this matter. Perhaps we know of the small percentage of alcoholic recovery from psychotherapy. Sometimes at the tables we hear a member recall how medicine or psychiatry failed to sober his or her life, until they found the AA program. These stories are always personal, and reveal more often the con game we were playing with ourselves. Alcoholics frequently use doctors to sober up their bodies in readiness for the next blast with the bottle. There are some doctors and psychiatrists who do not know they are treating an alcohol addict. Personal dishonesty sometimes camouflages either our symptoms, or our following treatment, or both. The AA fellowship counsels members honestly to seek proper professional help when needed, and does not enter into controversy within the professional field of alcoholism. AA stands as a life-style of personal recovery that works; as the record of recovering alcoholics in the fellowship shows.

Anyone who has known an AA member in the tragic history of his or her drinking years, and now knows the person in recovery, recognizes that this change is nothing short of a moral miracle. Only some five percent of addicts of other drugs in our new drug scene are rehabilitated successfully. Ethyl alcohol addicts used to be the lifelong losers. Continuing admission and acceptance along the way of the Twelve Steps of AA has brought us out of the tragedy.

Health-Giving Morale and Our Hope

At the start of the AA life-program the alcoholic's admission is always heavily negative. The alcoholic is withdrawing from the habit of long years of drinking, fighting a body chemistry addicted to a drug. This is the real agony of the beginner's "no" phase. It is a biochemical condition that needs good medicine, but it is far more than that. There is the dawning of the positive phase grounded in the alcoholic's negative admission, "I cannot drink." It is the search for the end of the physical and spiritual pain of the drunkard in the hope for recovery; the look from the abyss toward a possible manageable life, opening to concern and commitment to life. Simply, we cannot live with our drunken unmanageable selves. We want life. Amidst fears, frustration, alienation, we experience the human bottoming out of alcoholism, but with a difference that separates us from the emptiness of despair. There is purposeful hope in recovery.

It is difficult to verbalize the birth of the moral miracle of AA admission; difficult because its full reality is experienced when we have bottomed out in the dark night of our personal fall, as each person experiences it. It is the time of our personal awakening, our personality conversion. We have had enough of our drinking drive to what is really suicide, and look with serious hope to the better life. Hope is the central moral message of the AA program. It is a spiritual program, because it aims at putting human spirit back into the alcoholic's life. It is a moral program without being preachy. It inspires a health-giving morale.

Where does an alcoholic begin in admission with a sick body; a clouded brain; an emotionally disturbed, weak-willed, sometimes financially and socially broken life? AA admission centers on the spirit of a person through a lively faith and hope in oneself. Frequently, beginners are so disturbed in the chronic or even acute stages of alcoholism, that they cannot clearly reach beyond themselves. The first stages of admission are founded in admission of the need for help, understanding help. We may call out to God, but the cry is more plainly for God-inspired people, understanding people.

Our Fellowship

AA admission is always made in AA fellowship. This is why it is never just another futile alcoholic's admission, whenever the AA life-program is followed. Step One is never taken alone with one's fears in the darkness of alcoholic isolation. It is taken with fellow alcoholics, who experienced my dread, my forlorn spirit, my sick body, my search for hope amidst the progression of the disease of alcoholism. In the fellowship we understand and we care, and this understanding and this care inspires faith and hope in our new member.

The alcoholic's fear of dependence, as an attack on his or her ego, is especially understood by fellow alcoholics in their first steps of recovery. The AA policy of not forcing help on the alcoholic who refuses help and of giving him or her time, is sometimes badly misunderstood. *The alcoholic must want help.* His or her attachment to independence is strongly motivated by a selfish sense of isolation. Fellow AA members know this syndrome. "Easy does it" is a must in the fellowship.

The AA admission, "I am an alcoholic," therefore, is never drawn out of painfully alienated consciousness. It is proclaimed in a chorus of admissions, in a community of alcoholics, in the togetherness of the fellowship. The weak, hesitant, nervous admission of the beginner is strengthened by fellow recovering alcoholics, who show the way in living testimony, that they can make their admission in strength, conviction and success. And so the moral miracle of recovery is passed on.

Every drinking alcoholic is on an ego trip. Within the fantasy world of his or her own ego, the alcoholic is hopeless. Self-made promises to reform always turn into empty promises no matter how grandiose they may appear and no matter how inspiring the circumstances; whether they are made to one's family, one's clergyman, or an employer eager to help. Will power of itself is meaningless to the drinking alcoholic, too addictively active for the next drink. AA admission is never made as a strictly personal dynamism, a do-it-yourself technique. AA admission is efficacious through the fellowship by the Higher Power.

Every Twenty-Four Hours

AA admission is clearly not a completed, dated, verbal declaration. Of course, we can say that we first admitted our illness on a certain date. But this is not the context of our admission today. Admission grows in us in our acceptance of the AA program. This is the essence of our genuine admission. It is an on-going process, and must be on the level of a renewed twenty-four hour acceptance. We avoid easy universal pledges: "I'll never drink again." As the life of the recovering alcoholic matures in sobriety and the good life, his or her admission becomes daily enriched in the discovery of true self. We experience new blessings as well as new risks to our way of life. There are days when admission comes easily in a "no" to drinking and a "yes" to sobriety. But there are days when unexpected risks and uneasiness may very well appear. Admitting this AA style of living is an on-going acceptance of life. As is true of all life, no two twenty-four hours are quite the same. Daily reading of the brief recollections of the *Twenty-Four Hours a Day* book helps us.

Part of the learning art of AA is to make members aware of the reality of living twenty-four hours of personal admission. Our admission cannot linger in the past or leap into the future. It belongs to the now, the present, actually living life. Many a recovering alcoholic is deterred from genuine twenty-four hour admission by getting involved in the past or the future. How often we hear members say at the meeting: "I thank the Higher Power for this twenty-four hours of sobriety." Every fall from sobriety involves a fall from vigilance of the now. We do not have our fall in the past or in the future. It comes in the now. We must keep it that simple. Hindsight and foresight are secondary to the recovering alcoholic's insight, into action this day.

Although every genuine AA admission is an admission of hope in a life-long acceptance of total sobriety, we do not indulge in grandiose promises that we will never drink again. We know the emptiness of such presumptuous alcoholic promises. They presume an on-going strength. Actually we must work for that strength and that means to work in this twenty-four hours. We are ready to undertake the task of total sobriety, so long as we strive to keep this twenty-four hours sober. It is more than jolly power. Our power is not in our strength of will, but in the Higher Power inspiring us in our fellowship. This is the Power with us now, and which we hope will be with us by respecting our fidelity today. We can lose it, as some sadly do. We never just slip, we deliberately fall. The program is slip proof in the growth of maturity. But we must be aware of the risks.

The recovering alcoholic never really leaves the First Step in the acceptance of admission. There is no one cured of the disease, so that admission is a past event. Undoubtedly this is one reason why matured members like First Step tables. Admission pervades all the other steps. In fact, no AA Step is ever finished and complete. The term "step" can be misleading if it is taken to mean mere locomotion, as a step in walking. Every step in life is more than a timed event in a spaced journey. We do not know life's road map that well. Rather, the steps are qualitative steps in a recovering alcoholic's history, a career in sobriety in the good life. They are on-going steps in the moral evolution that constantly unfolds anew in the continuing progress of the program in life.

Admission deepens in the development of the other eleven steps. We shall explore this theme in the remaining chapters on the Twelve Steps. Especially in Steps Two and Three admission matures when we focus attention on belief that a Power greater than ourselves could restore us to sanity and make our decision to turn our wills and our lives over to the care of God, as we understand Him. Admission opens up a

97

healing faith in our very earthly lives. Everyday admission is a mission to the unending discovery of identity, knowing myself a little more. We are building the human in us.

IX. THE HIGHER POWER

Lack of power, that was our dilemma. We had to find a power by which we could live, and it had to be a Power greater than ourselves. Obviously. But where and how were we to find this Power? Alcoholics Anonymous.

Membership in AA has one basic requirement: the desire to stop drinking. We are talking about the alcoholic's desire to stop activating the disease of alcoholism. New members come to AA encumbered by fears and perplexities, skin deep in tragedy, eager to talk about their alcoholic problems. They know they are bottoming out, and they are anxious to share the experiences of men and women who have regained meaningful sobriety. They are in search of the power to recover. But many are astounded when they are told that the AA Steps constitute a moral program centered on God. What has Divine Power to do with recovery power? Resentment, the number one destroyer of the alcoholic, easily springs into action. Fortunately, this reaction is understood in the fellowship, even anticipated.

Resentment of God and a moral program appear in a variety of forms. People come to AA trying to step out of the wet set for the one motive of self-preservation. Many live in practical indifference to God, and take morality lightly in their own self-propelled search for pleasure and freedom. They feel unprepared to commit themselves to a God-centered program. They do not want to get holy. All they want is to get well. They prefer to stay on the human level and rid themselves of the pain of their disease. It does not take them long to realize that they have come to the right place to air these difficulties.

Still others regard God and morality as a matter of church affiliation, their confessional belief. They may even be active church members, but this role, as they experienced it, did not help them maintain sobriety. And so they seek out AA, but they do not come to discuss godly topics. They are looking for a program to stop drinking. Of course, there is some moral talk to be expected. But they are more attracted to AA by its winners, perhaps men and women whom they have known in their drinking days, who have learned a way of sobriety. They want to share in this know-how technique. For them it is a down-to-earth, not a heavenly venture.

Crisis-Awakening

Every alcoholic in his or her drinking career can hardly be classified as living a God-centered life. Obviously we were not practicing that belief in all of our affairs. Our moral *dis-ease* made us uncomfortable in any real concern and commitment to God and morality. Quite unlike us, the ancient Greeks believed that intoxication was a way of divine communion. But their gods were different from the loving God, who is not approached in this way. Alcoholism has its own way of deterring us from God. In various ways it corrupts active belief, and in some cases manages to destroy it. Obviously, in our permissive society there are many ways of weakening and destroying active belief in God. For many alcoholics, however, this sickness has its own way of becoming a graveyard of belief. How strange that AA should use the crisis of alcoholism as an awakening experience of Divine Power to inspirit our lives!

AA does not allege to have sophisticated proof for the existence of God. After all, one does not really find God at the conclusion of an argument, nor does one really lose God there. The Divine Power, as we understand Him, is a hallowed Presence in life. People who believe in a proved God generally have their belief in their proof rather than in God. God is really believed in through experience, the life of grace and nature. AA shows the alcoholic how he or she simply needs the Divine Power to manage a humanly unmanageable life. It is, for us, a crisis-awakening.

We experience the healing power of the fellowship, and we come to know that it comes with belief in a loving God. This is the God who still believes in us. Few of us experience the sudden strong awakening recorded by Bill in *Alcoholics Anonymous*. For most of us it is a gradual discovery of Divine Power in the recovering lives of our fellow alcoholics in AA. We want to share in that healing influence. In essence, it is a very human encounter of a person in need, thoroughly pragmatic, vitally useful, and selfish in the sense that it means recovery for us.

In the language of the Second and Third Steps: "We came to believe that a Power greater than ourselves could restore us to sanity." "We made a decision to turn our will and our lives over to the care of God as *we understood Him.*" No matter how prepared a member is to believe in God, a certain crisis preparation takes place before he or she, as an alcoholic, comes to believe *out of vital alcoholic recovery need.* This is a special kind of spiritual awakening among the varieties of spiritual experiences. Belief and surrender arise out of the depths of the alcoholic's powerlessness and unmanageability. Understanding this approach is paramount to appreciation of the words of the Third Step . . . "to turn our will and our lives over to the care of God *as we understood Him.*"

On the first reading we may take this to mean our personal way of understanding God, for example, in our confessional beliefs. This, of course, is true for alcoholics who have a confessional belief. Practicing the AA Steps in many cases activates our religious beliefs. However, there is a special meaning here for recovering alcoholics. Recovery experience in AA takes place by God, as we understand Him precisely as recovering alcoholics. There is a very personal experience of God as the Higher Power to help us amidst the crisis of the alcoholic's life. Again we stress this as a special kind of spiritual awakening commonly experienced in AA's Second and Third Steps.

"God as We Understood Him"

There is a dynamism at work in us from God as our Higher Power, higher than the power of alcohol that had been the power in our lives, higher than our power of self-propelled pride, and our ego-fantasies. This is the giving, loving God the recovering alcoholic is discovering anew out of crisis. It is the care of God "as we understood Him." There are indeed varieties of godly experience. Among these, the experience of the recovering alcoholic is a special experience, very personal in each one of us, of the loving care of God, who believes in us. We come to see there is far more of Him believing in us than our tiny bit of wisdom in believing in Him.

Before our crisis-awakening of a loving God, who cares, we may have feared God, the Great Avenger, the wrathful Judge. In our drinking alcoholic lives we may have feared this Great Avenger, as if He were penalizing us into ruination for our drink-driven lives. We may have even despaired of Him in our ever deepening chaos, which we may have taken as a sign of Divine Retribution. For some this meant a turning away from this sort of God. In some cases a clergyman not knowledge-able in alcoholism may have intensified our resentment in his plea that we take the pledge absolutely never to drink again out of fear of the Divine Wrath.

There was little or no experience of the God of Love, the forgiving God who guides the recovering alcoholic through each twenty-four hours. And as it worked out, this pledge, too, was powerless over alcohol. Through AA we now rediscover the power of a forgiving, loving God each day at a time. The fellowship, in genuine belief and real surrender, brought home to us the reality of this healing truth.

For many of us, our crisis-awakening was a real shock out of a shallow religion of routine ritual, a sort of Sabbath herd culture, that we performed out of habit. We were awakened into a real life encounter of Divine Power. We no longer prayed only because people do that sort of thing Sunday mornings in churches. We prayed daily because of a vital need

102

for strength from the Power, higher than the ruthless power that was wrecking our lives. Our lives were becoming more manageable by living the AA program grounded in belief in and surrender to God. In our lives before our crisis-awakening, we may have talked about the good God. Now we are experiencing the action of His goodness. We are not claiming any direct revelation of the heavens opening up. God as we understand Him is encountered in His works, in the action of recovery. This is a recovery needed by a sick world in general, and it is our experience in our particular variety of spiritual awakening in alcoholic recovery.

Out of the Depths

When an alcoholic is bottoming out in the acute throes of the disease, he or she can go on hopelessly in the progression of the disease or experience an awakening toward recovery. Many do play their own style of Russian roulette with the disease. They opt for a kind of stoic despair. Many also turn to hope in recovery, and for a great many of us this means the AA way of life. This means more than abstinence from alcohol. It means a moral rearmament, value changes, character transformation, gut-level change of long embedded habits. Alcoholic thinking, the next drink, alibis, lying, resentments, false pride, all these must give way to a healthy productive perspective for the action of living. There are, of course, numerous motivational therapies that endeavor to effect this building of the human in us. AA has come up with the most successful, through active recovery belief and personal surrender to the all-understanding God.

Bottoming out is a crisis, but it may not be a crisis-awakening to recovery. There must be *an all-encompassing relation to recovery* in this total disease of alcoholism. This can be achieved in the person, who opens his or her life to *the all-encompassing power of God.* For most of us, medicine can mend our sick bodies, psychology can help in guiding us to normal behavior, but the spirit of a person in a life-style of

103

recovery is best achieved in an all-caring, God-centered morality. We are talking about a recovery that aims at arresting an incurable disease involving a total person, and not just a phase of a person's existence.

We cannot overemphasize that we are talking about a variety of spiritual experience, which is a way of recovery. The process affects us bodily because the body has a marvelous capacity to recover when we have spirit, value and purpose in our lives. It can aid and ripen the health that good medicine restores. It affects us psychologically even more deeply, because we are restoring meaningfulness to our existence. Here is real ego-strength in personal worth repairing the damages of years of alcoholic ego-fantasy. Obviously, we are not talking about a hallelujah game.

This spiritual awakening comes in our shock at the depths of our alcoholic crisis. We are shocked by fear of the gathering gloom of crisis, but more than that we are shocked by the vital discovery of hope gradually unfolded in the lives of others in the AA fellowship, and in our own honest following of the program. We come to experience Divine Aid in being human again. All of this is difficult to relate. It is easy to share in the communion of AA experiences.

The God of love builds the human better than any human because He created the human out of love. In the spiritual transformation effected in the AA Second and Third Steps, this personal awakening is brought home to us in a loving experience of care and commitment revealed in the lives of fellow AA members who come to reach us at the AA meetings and personal contacts. And finally it is brought home to us in our own character change to the good life. The grace of God builds the human in honesty, humility, reverence for life and joy of sobriety. Grace never destroys us in fear of God, alienation, frustration and the psychic shocks of pseudo-religion.

Anyone who supposes we are dealing with emotional fantasy, a form of self-hypnosis in inventing aid from on high, is not talking about AA gut-level reality-therapy. AA does not exist as an experiment in some form of esoteric extrasensory perception. It is a fellowship of alcoholics recovering by belief in and surrender to God, as we alcoholics understand Him, in continuing steps of recovery. We know that it works, and we also know that to some it is incredible. There are some sincere disbelievers, who cannot accept any part of spiritual awakening because of their unquestionable faith in the supposed death of God in modern life, which they define on their own assumptions.

In the Union of Soviet Socialist Republics, there is widespread alcoholism. But the Soviets cannot employ AA, because they have a state policy that God is a fiction. Actually AA language of "the Higher Power" would be weak motivational therapy for them, since in the minds of many comrades the State is "the Higher Power," and that is, at least in part, why they are drinking. In Copenhagen, Denmark, there is great appreciation of medical care for the alcoholic, and the need for a moral program. Popular indifference to God makes a meaningful moral program difficult. There must be some active relation to God as the Higher Power. One does not get the power from do-nothing concepts of God! For all our faults, there remains in the American spirit of achievement some vital active belief in God. AA gives testimony to this fact. We live in an era of groping search for spiritual values, notwithstanding all the devaluing.

Bottoming out, for most of us in alcoholism, means the descent from the fun-loving drinker to the dregs of the sick alcoholic. Of course, we were sick long before we came to admit it. No two of us really bottomed out in the same way, although all of us had the inner shakes of our impending crisis. It is sometimes hazardous to compare bottoming out in any one-to-one relation. What would be a trip to the depths for one would be considered mild for another. So, too, ways of coming to spiritual awakening vary sharply. What awakens one person to the recovery power of a loving God might appear to be thoroughly unmoving to another. Some of us eagerly take the Second and Third Steps of the program in responding to belief in and surrender to God in rebuilding the human in us. Others fight these Steps with suspicion and distrust. It is surprising how some feel quite alien and strange in the simple honesty of loving and being loved.

The New Understanding

Many of us took God for granted and practiced our religion in a routine herd culture with no concern or commitment. Religion as we practiced it, if we really bothered to at all, did not interfere with our drinking. Perhaps we did believe in the good God, but we have used His goodness as a crutch for our drinking. Bottoming out in our spiritual awakening means the end of all this false jolly power, and turning on to the vital truth of the Higher Power in integral living. AA for us means a new understanding of the action of belief in our lifework of recovery.

AA gradually awakened us from a practical agnosticism, or from a God of fear, or from taking the good God for granted by implanting a new healing belief in us. This is not the same as saying that we adopted a new religion. Rather, it connotes a newness in our lives, the newness of honestly accepting God in our lives. This means that we are living our belief in God. For some this means to take their religion seriously. For others it means no more than taking God seriously. For all of us it means the way of moral recovery, which is far broader and deeper in meaningfulness than physical sobriety.

The great sober majority can understand God, as we understand Him, in some form of crisis experience, but not in the same vital meaning of AA people, who have walked in the alcoholic's valley of death. The recovering alcoholic has his or her own special recovery from gradual alcoholic suicide, alcoholic lying, pride, lust, avarice into life worth living in honesty, temperance, love, humility. It is a real life experience shared in the fellowship. It tells a brighter, more hopeful and positive story than the dreary, negative drunkalogue that some people falsely characterize as the delirious diet of AA groups.

It is sometimes said at the tables of AA meetings: "I thank God that I am an alcoholic." This is no gratification for the alcoholic disease. It is sincere thanksgiving for AA awakening to the human need of God, which so many try to escape from in a variety of masquerades. And we were past-masters, in the best W.C. Fields manner, of this disguise. Our crisis, which could have led us to insanity or death, became, for us, a discovery in our sickness of a healing faith, a sickness which is a little bit of the total sickness of the human family.

Recovering alcoholic clergymen are particularly equipped to express this new understanding. They recall how AA prepared them for entrance to active belief and the decision to surrender to a healing faith. They knew the theology of a loving God, but they also knew their drive to drink. They may have preached eloquently to others, but they had not changed their lives. In AA their lives are graced with a vital sobriety. A complex of causes work together in this healing: the shock of hitting bottom; the strikingly good example of recovering alcoholics in the fellowship who had been actively addicted for years; the earthy counsel in an honest day-by-day drive for sobriety; the joy of achieving — all grounded in the action of the simple love of God working throughout the Steps of recovery.

Self-Surrender

This is perhaps the most misunderstood word in the program. The new understanding that comes in the Second Step in admitting active belief in the Power of recovery, leads us to the Third Step — surrender to the Power. It is a Step that begins with real conflict, often the conflict of misunderstanding, and the refusal to accept what is understood. After years of heavy self-indulgence it is difficult to experience self-surrender. Many of us are sharply shocked into it. At the start we can easily mistake this step as self-abdication rather than self-surrender. We may come to think that it means confession that we are total failures, all bad.

Actually, it should be an experience of the good in us, seeking for what is better. It is a strengthening of our ego in the action of recovery, rather than utter admission of our nothingness. It does not call for complete passivity, a do-nothing attitude, because whatever we do is bad, and a silent waiting for God to do it all. What is really happening here is surrender of the self-centered drunk, centered around the glass, and instead putting God at the center of the action. This is a genuine ego-awakening, self-actualization, and not a requiem. It is really surprising what gross misunderstanding is experienced in taking this Step.

Many of us at this point suffer a maladjustment to will power. AA does not undersell will power. It does undersell the myth of will power that the addict can recover on his own will to sobriety. In this Step we make an admission of surrender to open our will power to the strong motivation of the Divine Will for us, and we do so in the belief that the Divine Will energizes us in a continuing creation. This new understanding in the action of surrender propels recovery of the new person in us. It is a daily continuing process, the fresh start of a lifework, that we must work at every twenty-four hours. It is the gateway to the remaining nine steps, as we shall see.

What we surrender is no glorious gift to God. It is our frailty, our weak wills, our downgraded life. We realize that our self-propelled will has only led along the pathways of our drive to drink, the nightmare of our compulsive will. It is principally our own old self that we turn over to the Higher Power, to empower us with the will to a newly discovered self. As we continue working the remainder of the steps, our surrender deepens and broadens into our lives. We decide to begin a surrender of life that entails the entire program.

Many of us are confused in the art of making this surrender. There is always the help of our fellow recovering alcoholics to come to our aid at a Third Step table. In their stories they encourage us by reflecting our difficulties, as they tell of their surrender. We must keep it simple for each twenty-four hours. Above all we must avoid grandiose images of surrender. In plain talk, it is the decision that we have loused up our life by drinking because of our bad character traits, and we ask God simply to direct us. When the strong drive to drink arises, we do not turn on our will power, which has repeatedly failed us, but humbly and simply ask God to control our "no" to drink. It is open response to the Higher Power. God is helping us keep it that simple. This is also the case in asking God to cool our anger, and quiet our resentments. We believe that the blueprint of God's help for us is in living the AA program. We are asking Him to empower us to live the AA Steps. By ourselves we are too weak. We let go of running the show and let God pilot our lives.

The Higher Power

The Swiss psychiatrist Carl Jung supports the co-founders of AA in their basic belief that a spiritual conversion centers on a loving, caring God and is the mainspring for genuine recovery of the alcoholic. Dr. Jung, in a letter to Bill W. which referred to one of the AA members, observed that: "his craving for alcohol was the equivalent on a low level of the spiritual thirst of our being for wholeness, expressed in medieval language, the union with God." From his clinical experience with alcoholics, Jung believes that they are in a misdirected search for the peak experience of transcendence in the chemical high of alcohol.

It is by no means coincidental that alcohol, as indeed other drugs, enters into the rituals of the religions of mankind. In the alcoholic's perception, this search for God perception is not always evident, but it does appear noteworthy that on a low level, the all-encompassing dedication of the alcoholic to alcohol has similarities to the central value of the Divine in life-style. At the tables we sometimes hear AAs tell how the spirits inspirited their lives: "I offered my all for the drink." "I was searching for God in a bottle." "I was taken over completely. It was my Higher Power." In his letter to Bill W., Jung points out that the Latin word for alcohol is "spiritus." The origin of the word "whiskey" has the same meaning in Celtic.

It is a tradition among AA people to speak of God as "the Higher Power." This manner of speaking dates back to the early days of AA in the Thirties. It grew out of the AA experience that alcoholics need a Power greater than themselves to make it. "Higher Power" is an action word that connotes the dynamic relation between God and the alcoholic. God believes in us and helps us. This relation is dynamic not only on God's side, but also on ours. We are empowered to be strong in our weakness, to know ourselves as we are, and to do something constructive about it in a new way of life.

God energizes our lives, consoles our fears, quiets our resentments, our anger, and above all sobers our lives so long as we continue in our surrender to Him. This is not a passive, robot-like surrender that we talk about. It strengthens our ego in a proper sense. It is dynamic, because we actively turn our wills and our lives over to Him to be changed into a life worth living. God is to us the Power above all our finite frailties, stronger for us than our strong drive to drink, deeper in us than our inmost sensibility to carouse, more precious to us than all our years of attachment to the power of alcohol.

In ancient times men made a religion of their vices. The Greeks had Dionysius as the god of wine and the Romans had Bacchus. In our own way, we had made a god of our drink. It had become our life-dedication, the power in our life-story. Now it is all changed by our Higher Power, our God as we understand Him. Alcoholics do not find this all-out life dedication unusual. They have a way of centering a value in their lives.

Whereas before we lived in the obsession for drink, we now live in faith and hope and love of the Higher Power. We can paraphrase the words of the Psalmist: "Out of the depths, we have cried to you O Lord." "O Lord you brought me up from the nether world; you preserved me from among those going down into the pit." It is a mystery why we drank, and it is a God-given mystery why we stop. The Divine builds the human in us. Truly, when the alcoholic uncovers and faces this need, there is unlocked a psycho-spiritual conversion. This amounts to a vital shift from negative to positive life values. This is the core of AA therapy, as Dr. Harry Tiebout, the first psychiatrist to study AA, came to realize.

X. THE PROCESS OF PERSONAL RECOVERY

A.A.'s Twelve Steps are a group of principles, spiritual in their nature, which, if practiced as a way of life, can expel the obsession to drink and enable the sufferer to become happily and usefully whole.
Twelve Steps and Twelve Traditions

By now the reader should be amply informed that the core of the alcoholic's recovery is not in a body restored to health, but in a personal spirit of sobriety. Let us review again some basic understandings. Understanding the recovering alcoholic, of course, implies understanding the need for medical help. So, too, psychological counsel is important for acquiring the mentally healthy spirit of sobriety. But this is only the beginning. Alcoholics must be aware that their problem does not end when they leave the hospital, or sanatorium, or the private care of a physician or psychiatrist.

Some infective diseases end after treatment. The patient is cured. Addictive alcoholism is not one of these diseases. It can always be activated by drinking. And the patient, to remain well, must observe total sobriety amidst a culture that is getting wetter. In 1935 at Akron, Ohio, Alcoholics Anonymous began as the outcome of meetings between a well-known surgeon and a New York broker. Both were severe cases of alcoholism. Their program in Twelve Steps was designed for living, to maintain sobriety in the life of the addictive alcoholic. Its success is now legendary in America.

These Twelve Steps guide the process of personal recovery. Personal recovery is a process rather than a completed event, because it is on-going as a style of life. It pertains to personal recovery rather than to mere bodily recovery because it aims at maintaining the spirit of sobriety in the alcoholic person. Furthermore, it is personal because each person lives the program in the particular conditions of his or her own life and according to the quality of sobriety they are achieving. Some

112

attain a high quality of sobriety that is productive in their own lives and reaches out to influence others deeply. Others attain a good sobriety that is enduring and is encouraging to others. Many of us mediate between these two groups, but what is important is that we are endeavoring to live the Twelve Steps of recovery.

The Twelve Steps of Alcoholics Anonymous

Step One — "We admitted we were powerless over alcohol — that our lives had become unmanageable."

Step Two — "Came to believe that a Power greater than ourselves could restore us to sanity."

Step Three — "Made a decision to turn our will and our lives over to the care of God *as we understood Him.*"

Step Four — "Made a searching and fearless moral inventory of ourselves."

Step Five — "Admitted to God, to ourselves, and to another human being the exact nature of our wrongs."

Step Six — "Were entirely ready to have God remove all these defects of character."

Step Seven — "Humbly asked Him to remove our shortcomings."

Step Eight — "Made a list of all persons we had harmed, and became willing to make amends to them all."

Step Nine — "Made direct amends to such people wherever possible, except when to do so would injure them or others."

Step Ten — "Continued to take personal inventory and when we were wrong promptly admitted it."

Step Eleven — "Sought through prayer and meditation to improve our conscious contact with God *as we understood Him,* praying only for knowledge of His will for us and the power to carry that out."

Step Twelve — "Having had a spiritual awakening as the result of these steps, we tried to carry this message to alcoholics, and to practice these principles in all our affairs."

These Twelve Steps charter the process of personal recovery as we find it in AA. They are evidently not a hospital type of recovery. Alcohol is mentioned only once explicitly in the Steps, in Step One. The Steps are not a way of sobering up from an alcoholic bout or bender. They constitute a style of life of on-going recovery, preventative of the activation of alcohol addiction through total sobriety of a moral quality. The Twelve Steps are a life-program for the addictive alcoholic, who is never cured, but is recovering by maintaining a sober way of life.

As alcoholism once spread its disintegration in all our affairs, so now in recovery we are to practice recovering principles in all our affairs. The Twelve Steps are a vital antidote against the total disease of alcoholism that insidiously victimized the addicted alcoholic bodily and spiritually, individually and socially. The AA program is a recovery philosophy or ethics of life, rather than a way or a medicine or a technique of psychology in any professional sense. It is a life-program instituted by recovering alcoholics, which experience shows successful when practiced.

We have already dealt with the first three Steps leading into the program which give the recovering alcoholic the mainspring for action. Honest admission to an alcoholic identity and daily acceptance of the role of the meaningful "no" to the first drink and the lively "yes" to a sobriety of a moral quality constitute the foundational First Step for continuing on in the program. The Second and Third Steps bring us to the *active* belief and the will to surrender to the Higher Power. Here is the core of our recovery power, to arrest the weakness of our disease and effect the total building of the human in our lives.

In AA experiences, we are now moving in the dynamics of recovery. Our will power and our lives are becoming more manageable to move on. Life is change, motion. We are never static. We either move forwards or backwards, upwards or downwards. We have known the backward and downward motion of our active alcoholism. Now we are on the move forward and upward. What is important is that we do not consider our recovery complete, and that we have no more problems. If we should believe this, we have a problem.

There are new members who believe that they have made the whole program in the First Step. Somehow they leap to the Twelfth Step to announce it to the world, and the campaign to dry up all drunks is on. They are the jolly green giants, who do the program in two steps, the "two steppers." The mouth that roared booze at the bar is now roaring victory at the table. Sometimes these people are generous enough to sound off loud belief in and a louder surrender to God. But these are hollow Second and Third Steps. They are staggering steps that paralyze the process of recovery.

Of course, it is characteristic of new members in general to have misunderstandings of the meaningfulness of the Steps, and to undergo some spirit of conquest and exhilaration. It is a most relieving experience to unburden oneself of the mad nightmare of active alcoholism and to experience purposeful living again. Every new member has his or her honeymoon in AA. In time we come down from cloud nine and walk the rugged earth again. What is important is that we do not fall off our cloud by mistaking our newfound strength as the strength to drink again; or descend by way of an emotional flight from the highs to the lows of a spiritless sobriety — flat, dull and unprofitable — the dry drunk syndrome.

Recovery Through Self-Discovery

When we have matured enough in the program, when we begin to feel comfortable in the steps we have taken, and this takes a matter of some months, we should on advice of our sponsor or another experienced AA member move on to the Fourth Step. Our admission now moves on, strengthened by our Higher Power, to face our lives, our inner selves. "Know thyself." We come to Step Four: "Made a searching and fearless moral inventory of ourselves." This is more than the interior reflection made in Step One, which centers on the admission of alcoholic identity. It is more than an admission of

115

our general moral liabilities. It is also admission of our moral assets, our good qualities already evidenced in our self-honesty in Step One, and in our belief in and will to surrender to God, our Power of recovery, as we advanced in the Second and Third Steps.

We have already experienced what we can do for our return to the integrated life. We have many assets to note as well as liabilities. This is important for the recovering alcoholic, because it would indeed be depressing simply to turn to his or her degrading qualities of the drinking years. The moral inventory is meant to assess one's good qualities, built on the goodness in us, with the liabilities that obsessed us not only in our drinking days, but which were there before and prepared us for our fall and linger on in modified ways. A proper perspective of what the moral inventory is can really make us want it. Too often we regard it as merely dreaded exposure to our failures, and so we put it off. Nothing could be further from the truth. More members would gladly take the moral inventory if they came to see it in its proper light.

It is true that every AA member is making a moral inventory at the tables. As we tell our story and listen to stories told around the tables of successes and failures, we are morally reflecting on ourselves. But there is more to the Fourth Step than this. It is a studied, concentrated search of ourselves, done at a special time, in which we list our moral assets and liabilities. Some write out their moral inventory, and this is to be preferred as a more studied way of reflection. Others do it mentally. Either way we should be aware of the danger of turning it into a remorseful reflection. We must keep the proper perspective of the inventory in our mind, because moral means the good and bad in us and not just the bad.

In our interior search for our moral liabilities, we do not mean just our moral weaknesses when we drink, but those that characterize our life in general, and which eventually bring us to drinking when they remain unchecked. These are our angers, resentments, envies, and jealousies in our low times. They are our complacencies, our over-confidence in the high times of our successes. We must take the view from the center of our life, how we relate to ourselves, to God, to people, to sex, money, work, possessions, and security in terms of what is good and bad for us. Our moral defects of character are, of course, unbottled in our drinking, but they are somehow there deep in our character, in our total life-style. They can bring us back to drinking again or lead us into a sorry kind of sobriety. For example, it may be a grandiose pride in being a winner that keeps us sober, our old pride now masquerading in another disguise.

The moral inventory should never be an exercise in self-righteousness. True, we list our good points, but we are deeply concerned with self-knowledge of our moral defects, defects that may be escaping us because we fear to expose them in real self-honesty. In his work on the Twelve Steps, co-founder Bill cites seven capital moral defects, the seven deadly sins: pride, greed, lust, anger, gluttony, envy, sloth. Except for gluttony, they are broader than alcoholism. We can recognize them in our lives in our non-drinking years, but they really exploded in our drinking careers.

We were gluttons for our own fleshy selves and then for our drink motivated by self-pride. We wanted things our way and in our time. We lusted after the pleasant feelings in our greed for self-satisfaction, ridden with anger when things did not go our way, envious of people who had it made, and filled with sloth about really doing anything to make ourselves better people. These moral traps were deeply inbuilt into our lives, and perpetuated by our addictive drinking. They do not just disappear. A fearless searching moral inventory, to bring them to the surface for the sake of ensuring their control, is essential to genuine recovery.

Some people can live in a recovery that is more physical than moral. However, real personal recovery is alive in genuine humility, the warmth of love, the balance of emotional temperance, the regulation of prudence, and good practical common sense. These are the fruits of a true moral inventory. It is always an inventory for the action of recovery of the whole person. The Fourth Step is a step into humility, the humility of self-knowledge for action, action that takes time.

Self-Discovery in Depth

Each Step evokes our personal response. We react to things. We respond to persons. The response of the Fourth Step comes in the Fifth Step: "Admitted to God, to ourselves, and to another human being the exact nature of our wrongs." Growth in the surrender of our lives to God means that we admit our past failure in keen awareness of the wrongness of our lives. We admit that it was wrong for us personally and that our lives wrongly related to our fellow human beings. The person we choose to tell this to should be one who understands, someone we have taken into our intimacy. This may very well be our sponsor, or another AA member, a friend, doctor or clergyman.

Confession is good for the human spirit, to unburden ourselves, to release long pent-up fears, to quiet anxieties. We try to sum up the story of our personal wrongness of character, its exact nature as best we can. Drinking is not the full story of our wrongness of life. The person we are in our moral foibles has a great deal to do with it. Humble confession to another person before God is a great antidote to our number one defect, our pride. To achieve it is a great step in recovery. For many, this Step is a real awakening to the dignity of our personal worth, the vital value of God to us and a step toward rebuilding the human with others.

The person with whom we make the Fifth Step should be an understanding listener. More than that, he or she should be a helpmate in our inventory; an intimate in our life-story can help us in recollection. A capable sponsor or another experienced AA member can be especially resourceful in relating to us out of his or her experience in making the Fifth Step, and particularly guide us from our fears and the danger of falling into remorse. The moral inventory is not a backward motion into a tragic past. It should serve us like the driver's mirror in a car, to guide our forward motion in recovery.

Spiritual Readiness

Step Six is a Step of readiness. "Were entirely ready to have God remove all these defects of character." Our moral inventory furnished us with a more complete understanding of what is to be done in our life for our personal recovery. By Divine help we aim at accomplishing this life work. We realize that our strength for recovery is not principally in our will power, but in a Higher Power. We are ready to respond to Him, not as if He will do all, and we will be utterly passive. Our readiness is a readiness to enliven our lives for the good. It is by His Power that we act; for left to ourselves, we are not ready, we procrastinate.

Step Six is open to easy misinterpretation if we forget the important word "ready." The Step does not call for the *actual* removal of *all* our defects. If this were done, the process of recovery would be ended, and there would be no need for the other Steps. The Step is really a continuation of humility. It signals our moral readiness to act on our moral inventory, not by ourselves, but by Divine aid. The aim of the Step is ideal. It declares our readiness to rid ourselves of our character defects. It is another way of asserting our will for the good life. What we do in this Step centers on practicing humility.

In our daily lives we work at honest openness to Divine aid, and strive to abandon our alcoholic thinking of defeatism and our pride in doing it "my way." One might say that for some this is the most neglected of all the Steps. One can pass over it lightly. We, who were ever ready for the next drink, ever ready to hasten our own selfish quests, now practice a spirit of preparedness to open up our lives to God, and we do this best by opening up to those around us. Our drinking alcoholic years made us prisoners within our own skins. We are more ready now to listen, to be understanding of others, to be more patient, compassionate, helpful in our daily tasks with others.

The Humble Petition — No Humbug

Step Seven: "Humbly asked Him to remove our shortcomings" is intimately connected with Step Six. Out of our readiness for Divine aid comes the petition, the request that God help us. Of course, this petition pervades all the Steps. But it is time now to concentrate on it. The alcoholic is especially equipped for demanding rather than asking, and least of all for humbly asking. Too often our prayer in the past was a demand for what we wanted, rather than a humble request to do what God wants for us. We were not asking for help. We were dictating it. Notwithstanding the many humiliations of our drinking days, we had not learned to be humble. We feared humility, because we never understood it. We had to learn that only the strong can be really humble. And we were weak. Humility is grounding our identity, knowing our place, and taking it. Our genuine prayer for recovery is a prayer of hope, because we have found our place in the Seventh Step and we are taking it.

Our way of humbly asking God's help is a simple petition of hope in God and in ourselves through Divine aid. We need not resort to long formal prayers. We need only quietly ask for the help in our needs, the need for strength to continue to say "no" to the first drink, and the need to learn to live with our shortcomings, and at the same time strive to control and gradually work to remove them. We cannot expect instantaneous recovery of the whole person. We must be temperate in our hopes, not expect too much of ourselves or of others in understanding our recovery. Our presumption and scruples die a hard death.

Prayer for patience should be a daily occurrence. And coupled with it there should be the prayer for a sense of humor. We recovering alcoholics are prone to take ourselves too seriously. Good humor can ease the way. After all, especially for those of us who were the life of the party, this should not be too difficult a role. It is a real blessing to be able to laugh at oneself. It is symptomatic of a good spirit in some of our overly serious role-playing.

XI.   STEPPING OUT OF OURSELVES

Happy are those who hunger and thirst for what is right:
they shall be satisfied. Matthew 5:6

In the beginning an alcoholic's recovery is very personal. However, as recovery advances we open up more and more to those around us. This entails an awareness of certain retribution to others, and the duty to make proper satisfaction. Many of us will probably never be able to repay our family, and especially our spouse, for the troubled years of ever-mounting grief and shame. There is the moral debt we owe our friends for repeated disappointments in us, for our infidelities.

Many, too, can include rash abuses of the good will of our employers, who believed in us enough to give us another chance. To all of these we owe some satisfaction for our alcoholic pathological lying. In an age so very sensitive to the physical pollution of the environment, it is curious how many of us can treat lightly our moral pollution of our human environment, our community, by the frequent bad example of our carousings. Finally, there may very well be monetary debts that we need to resolve.

Recovery Through Reparation

Certainly it is a very special kind of judgment that we sometimes hear at the tables: "I only hurt myself in my drinking and I can best repair that by practicing sobriety." Or again the specious observation: "People don't want to hear me say that I am sorry. They heard enough of that from me in the past. They do want to see me sober. Sobriety is my amendment to others." We like to tell ourselves that the AA program is a selfish program. How many times we have heard that said! And it is true, if we understand it properly. The alcoholic has to learn the proper habit of self-respect. But we can only do this by opening up to others. No man is an island. There is more than romantic poetry in our human togetherness.

122

In Step Eight we "Made a list of all persons we had harmed, and became willing to make amends to them all." It is preparatory to the actual work of recompensation. We must first of all have the personal willingness to repay our moral and physical debts to others. And we must make a prudent account of people we harmed. It should be evident that this is no easy task for the recovering alcoholic. It requires a definite condition of readiness in recovery. For years the drinking alcoholic has been neglectful of responsibilities to others. It has become part of his or her image. A successful breakthrough in this area is a definite sign of recovery.

It should be plainly evident why Alcoholics Anonymous, in working out the Steps, should assign a definite Step in preparation for recompensation. It takes a real strength of character to admit a moral debt to others after years of playing the game selfishly. AA experience realizes this Achilles' heel of the recovering alcoholic, and steadily prepares for it in the Steps. In fact, one can say that being in AA is a general way of showing to ourselves and to others that we are mending our ways.

In reflecting on the literal meaning of this Step, it could very well be that we are willing to make amends to everyone we harmed, but can we honestly list all of them? Is the Step too ideal? We may even imagine ourselves to be public enemy number one of our neighborhood and then some. Repayment is too heavy we tell ourselves. Let us recall, however, that the wording of this Step was written by recovering alcoholics, well aware of alcoholic thinking. The Step needs strong wording to produce action, to check putting it off.

Practically, it may be true that many of us cannot list all persons we harmed over many years, but we should try to make an honest survey as best as we prudently can. This is needed for the sake of putting meaning into our willingness to make amends to all. Once again we must be keenly aware that this is not a memory exercise in remorse, but a strong effort to put down our fears of the past, to make things right in justice to others. We should compose ourselves quietly and with pencil and paper go to it. We can enlist the aid of another as in Step Five in composing our list, if this would make us more comfortable.

Step Nine is the real test for good common sense. This involves the actual work of repayment. "Made direct amends to such people wherever possible, except when to do so would injure them or others." This calls for selecting from our list of persons we harmed, those who can be reached in the circumstance of our life and with an openness to our spirit of amendment so far as we can judge. It would be futile indeed to approach people whom we would only further anger, who would find us incredible, who would even make our efforts into a comic scene. The collective experience of AA testifies there are many people who are grateful for our efforts to apologize, to ask pardon humbly, and to try to make right whatever was our wrongdoing — moral, physical, or financial. We are, of course, not speaking here of amendment that is only legal by the letter of the law. Step Nine goes far beyond legal satisfaction to genuine personal amendment.

Frequently the advice and counsel of experienced AA members is not only helpful but badly needed. Some of us overkill the Ninth Step. It becomes an explosion of grandiose extravagance in seeking forgiveness, and even at times wrecking our financial lives in the haste of paying debts. There are instances, too, when we do serious injury to another in our amendments. We may have played the Don Juan in our active alcoholism. In our drive for amendment we need prudence not to disturb our own unsuspecting spouses over an affair of the past that would be better forgotten, or disturb another unsuspecting family in unsavory and really uncalled for disclosures. Like all the Steps, Step Nine is intended to build the human, not destroy it.

Understanding the recovering alcoholic is at times difficult for others in the process of making amends for past wrongs. It is the Step where the recovering alcoholic relates to others whom he or she has failed and neglected in the past. What is important is that others do not falsely generalize that all

124

alcoholics are irresponsible, and their will to make amends is at worst a caprice and at best only a hapless effort. The disease of alcoholism always brings damage to the alcoholic and this spreads to others. Genuine personal recovery must involve amendments. AA is living testimony of thousands of cases of sincere action in amendments.

Continuing Moral Inventory

Step Ten is a step into a reinforced life. It is a continuing self-evaluation Step. "Continued to take personal inventory and when we were wrong promptly admitted it." Although we have made our moral inventory in Step Four, there is need of a continuing self-evaluation of our assets and liabilities as we mature in our recovery. Step Four is a prolonged look in depth at ourselves. Step Ten continues to monitor our lives by brief reflections on our good and bad character traits. For many of us, this becomes a daily practice, preferable in quiet moments at the end of the day. Each twenty-four hours is different. A new day brings new insights into what is good and bad in us. The AA program has brought us a long way in the personal recovery of a moral quality of life control. The aim of this Step is to reinforce our progress by continual scrupulous self-examination.

Sometimes we hear it said at the tables: "I had a great day. There were no problems." Naturally, there is nothing wrong with experiencing an emotionally good day. But the judgment sometimes can be indicative of riding the clouds, of failing to know ourselves. Without shaking up our lives, we should be aware that every day has its problems as part of the game of life. There is always the hidden problem of the time-bomb of our alcoholism within us. There are character defects to check, which are there ready to be turned on. One can easily pick resentment, the number one offender of the alcoholic. It can lurk in our lives in subtle and elusive ways.

Character change in the process of recovery, becoming an integrated person, is a gradual process, a life story. This is why

AA seriously is for life. Each new day in the changes of life makes the picture somewhat different with new discoveries of the good, the new challenges of what is wrong. Promptitude in admitting our mistakes uncovered in our moral inventory is a real sign of advance in personality recovery. In our active alcoholism we were so artful in dodging admission of our mistakes. In our pride we are still tempted to do so.

The recovering alcoholic needs to give special vigilance to loneliness, fatigue and hunger. One can be lonely in a crowd, but not in community or a fellowship. Alienation from God, oneself, fellowman, and nature are especially evident in today's people, in all walks of life, in a variety of moods and modes. It appears in modern life in an anxiety experience that people cannot easily identify. It is a real shock that everybody is more or less aware of, the basic awareness of need, of care, of understanding. If used properly, such experiences can humble us, and open our lives more to God, ourselves, our fellowmen, and the world around us. Our on-going moral inventory is paramount to AA maturity and another step into personal recovery. What a paradox that we learn the art of being human more from our failures than successes, when we turn failure into good.

More Power for Action

Step Eleven is a real reinforcement in the art of integrated living. "Sought through prayer and meditation to improve our conscious contact with God *as we understood Him,* praying only for knowledge of His will for us and the power to carry that out." This is the Step that many of us never thought we could reach. Somehow, through living the program it reached us. We all can remember how as new members we looked lightly or not at all to God's role in our personal recovery. We may have thought a great deal about the doctor's pill-dispensing role when we were in the hospital or about our own will power role in recovery. Sobriety was a physical meaning; as physical and tangible as the drink that fouled us. Through AA we came to an active belief in God as the Higher Power, who gives us strength over our weakness. We came to understand our weakness as interior, more in our spirit, our morale, than in our body. We came to see our personal recovery as mainly spiritual in this context. It is no accident that AA groups choose to close a meeting with the "Our Father" prayer.

Many AA members come the hard way to discovery of the meaningfulness of prayer. The prayer that we rejected was for the most part our own prayer of hypocrisy, the help we asked for in our active alcoholism, which for so long we really did not want. It was useless because of the pray-er rather than the action of prayer itself. Prayer; the lifting of the mind and the heart to God too often was a formal routine that never advanced out of our childhood, never moved onward in personal maturity, especially emotional maturity. For many it was little more than a sentimental release. This is true of men as well as women. In total AA experience the recovering alcoholic grows in realistic prayer. By our frequent attendance at meetings we come to participate in the strength of prayer in the fellowship.

AA recoveries are alive in the strength of prayer as we open up our minds and hearts to the power of God. It comes to us as a cry out of the depths of our crisis-experience, our hitting bottom. It begins with us doing the petitioning, even demanding what we want, and how we want it. But as we grow in the spiritual program of the Steps, we come to listen more to what the will of God is for us in times of joy as well as sorrow. This comes in a genuinely humble, growing surrender to the will of God for us in our gradual awakening. The Spirit of the Higher Power in the fellowship is clearly our source of strength. In the Eleventh Step we concentrate on the dynamics of prayer.

The prayer of meditation is, for us, largely mental reflection on God's providence, the loving care God gives us in on-going recovery. A popular meditation from the Matt. Talbot Retreat is the application of the parable of the prodigal son to our lives. In this parable, God is pictured as a forgiving father who generously receives his son who only returns to him after

127

wasting his substance in prodigality. The alcoholic can easily identify as the prodigal son. The Matt. Talbot Retreat for the Recovering Alcoholic is an excellent opportunity for growth in the Eleventh Step of the AA program, to improve our conscious contact with God.

There are many ways of meditating in quiet times of reflection. Recovery offers us a variety of experiences of peace of mind, serenity, and the good life that manifests God's care of our lives in faith and hope and love. Centering the awareness of the presence of God in our daily lives is a vital dynamic in recovery. In the act of self-reflection, we come to take a prolonged look at God's will for us in our recovery, and we pray to understand it in a balanced view of our lives. We realize that we are far from perfect.

Our prayer moves past petition, talking to God about our needs, to the prayer of forgiveness, especially the grace to forgive ourselves. Finally, we come to the prayer of gratitude: We are grateful to God for our lives graced by so many blessings, for our family, our work, friends, the opportunities to do good, and the AA fellowship. AA people are replete with experiences that tell how their affairs improved greatly as they grew in contact with God in seasons of joy and grief.

There are, of course, dry seasons when prayer is difficult, but we learn to use the difficulty as a prayer of surrender to the Divine will. Our religion helps many of us in this effort. For others it is, in the main, their practice of AA self-honesty to the Higher Power. We know what we have gained by following the AA Steps; a real sense of belonging to the brotherhood of man under God. The world for us is no longer a hostile place and we are not alienated, fragmented in alcoholic fears and loss of purpose. We are ready now for the Twelfth Step, which is never a point of finality in the AA life journey, but rather a new beginning.

XII JOYFUL SOBRIETY IN
THE ART OF LIVING

Where there is hatred let me sow love;
Where there is injury — pardon;
Where there is doubt — faith;
Where there is despair — hope;
Where there is darkness — light, and
Where there is sadness — joy.
O Divine Master, grant that I may not so much seek . . .
to be understood as to understand . . .
Prayer of St. Francis of Assisi

The sincere endeavor of the recovering alcoholic to practice the Steps of the AA way of life brings him or her along the way of a personal discovery, which is a genuine spiritual awakening. We have come a long way from the fearful search for understanding to a matured growth of self-understanding. This joy of achievement inspires us to broaden and deepen our self-discovery in all our affairs at home, at work, and in our community.

As we have received freely from others in the AA fellowship, we are enlivened to pass on to others in need of this precious gift of personal recovery. Personal growth always needs fellow humans. This is particularly true of alcoholics, because their lives are especially damaged by alienation. It took us some time to realize this. In fact, personal recovery can easily be measured by generous response to the need to understand people in all our affairs. In the Twelfth Step, the recovering alcoholic especially matures in his or her understanding of the personal need to help fellow alcoholics.

Dynamics of Recovery

Step Twelve: "Having had a spiritual awakening as the result of these Steps, we tried to carry this message to alcoholics, and to practice these principles in all our affairs." Needless to point out, the moral miracle of AA is not to be discovered in reading the literal expression of the program in the Twelve Steps. It is a life-discovery in those who need the discovery and have endeavored to live it. There is always awkward difficulty in attempting to verbalize the personal experience of spiritual awakening, precisely because it is personal and even more so because it is spiritual.

In these times when so many people are enclosed in the world of material needs, prisoners within their own skins, they are more easily given to a material awakening to a better world by the wonder-chemistry of a pill or even the programmed technique of better body therapy. How often spiritual awakening is misunderstood as a sentimental trip to Hallelujah, as a sudden leap to euphoria, even as a crude testimony of the horrors of the sin of boozing sometimes heard in a drunkalogue. How many of us can recall our own false evaluations of spiritual awakening in such misunderstandings. As we progressed through the AA Steps we were gradually made conscious of the very human, even earthy dimension of our spiritual awakening. It became for us a response in life to a loving God, who inspired us to rebuild the human out of the damaged life of the drinking alcoholic.

Step by step through frequent attendance at the meetings we progressed in our admission of our alcoholic identity, and accepted new habits of living through a strong "no" to that first drink, and a lively "yes" to good living. Our awakening came by seeing God in godly inspired people, who were caught as we were in the self-assumed hopeless and unmanageable life of the addicted alcoholic. We were given hope in their action of recovery grounded in belief in a Higher Power, and we came to practice surrender of our fragile will and life to the Higher Power.

Our dynamics of personal recovery did not come without faltering steps, set-backs, and failures in our self-discovery. But we had the counsel and example of AA people, who had already experienced all these, and made it through to a comfortable, even joyful sobriety. We learned the need to take a seasoned hard look at our lives, to use our assets and repair our damage to self from bad traits of character, to make amends for our damage to others by making prudent amends.

We came to the gut-level understanding that alcoholics do not simply drink; instead they feed a sickness, activate a disease, take off on an ego-trip of resentments, alienation, and anxiety that is no more than a masqueraded suicide. We admitted this to God and to another fellow human, and we continued our personal inventory in the awareness that as life changes so we must keep morally vigilant to the changing scene. As we progressed, so in that measure we were genuinely humbled in prayer from proud dictation to surrender to God. We began to live a more actively human life, open to real personal need, especially to empathy for other fellow humans in the search of the gift that we had not earned, that was so freely given to grace our lives.

How difficult it is to sum up the meaning of our spiritual awakening! It is not possible to capsulate it in a formula, reduce it to a system of reasoning. It is more than a technique to be mastered; rather it is a way of life. At the beginning we thought that we awakened only to the human fellowhip of Alcoholics Anonymous, people who were winners in their conquest over the challenge of active alcoholism. It was a mission made possible by understanding people through the grace of God.

Gradually, we came to understand how very much we did not understand, the presence of the Power of the fellowship in a loving God. The secret of the fellowship was far deeper than human good will, far more enveloping than human together- ness. We came to experience the Life of all the living in our recovery to life through the fellowship. Our discovery was not easy. It began with a crisis-experience of active alcoholism. It matured through many misunderstandings and failures. There is still much for us to understand, but we have come to a way of continuing understanding of a loving God, of ourselves and others by more patient listening, by more prudent action.

In the Twelfth Step we proceed in spiritual awakening to concentrate on practicing AA principles in all of our affairs. It is an earth-bound, continuing, spiritual awakening. The time is now and the place is our world. Just as our alcoholism involved others in our dissipation, so our spiritual awakening in practicing our AA principles in all our affairs involves others in our recovery. First of all this influences our family. Since we took our First Step in AA this healing influence began. The family that was nearly deranged by our alcoholic madness, when honestly open to recovery, gradually grows in sharing the effects of our recovery. There is an ease in living, in hope for the future. As we meet our responsibilities of husband to wife, or wife to husband, parent to children, children to parent, the whole family benefits.

AA families who share in the recovery of an alcoholic are held together. There are countless cases of these successes. Often recovery entails a better economic life. In some cases financial damage is so severe that we must settle for less. However, in the moral strength of practicing AA principles, especially of honesty and humility, there is the strength of fidelity. How often the wife of a recovering alcoholic wistfully remarks: "We are thankful for his sobriety. Of course, things could be better, but life is so much more liveable now."

Recovering Our Family and Work

Practicing AA principles in our family brings home to us the truth that recovery in our lives entails more than our physical sobriety. It involves emotional sobriety. The recovering alcoholic husband or wife only achieves growing success in marriage and the family when they recover as total persons from their character defects. Frequently this means that they must grow in understanding their spouse and children, in regaining their confidence gradually, in tempering pride, in avoiding the drive to make others over into one's own image, in learning to give of oneself in patience and humility. Sobriety of itself is not the final answer to all familial difficulties. It is an important beginning. The recovering alcoholic has to face the problems common to families in today's society, particularly the rearing of children amidst the present youthquake. An Alateen group is of great service in responsive understanding of teenagers and the problems of the alcoholic's family.

After years of prolonged neglect, spouses have to make important readjustments in putting romance back into marriage. Attendance at open AA meetings and at an Al-Anon group helps a wife or husband understand their recovering spouse. However, there is a personal area of relationship here that only a husband and wife can restore in their intimate lifestyle. There is always the danger of judging the AA way of recovery jealously. Especially wives at times are prone to say "Why wasn't our love enough to make him maintain sobriety?" There is a real failure here in understanding the disease of alcoholism. It is far better to be grateful that the AA program is working in the restoration of marital love and family welfare.

At this point in recovery there is a shifting of roles in the whole recovering family. The spouse who had to take the place of the irresponsible alcoholic now finds it necessary to abdicate this role as the alcoholic assumes normal family functions. Some spouses find it difficult to step down. There is a failure of awareness as to what recovery entails in honesty and humility. So, too, the eldest son, who may have had to fill in the role of father for the younger children, now also finds that he is to step down as his father regains responsibility through sobriety. Al-Anon group counseling is very helpful in guiding families through pathways of new identities as recovery unfolds in an alcoholic's family.

Realistically, there are marriages that cannot be put together by alcoholic recovery. They have ended in divorce or separation. Recovery means that the alcoholic faces this fact, if he or she has not already done so, and accepts it in a sane and healthy way. In making the Ninth Step of amends, the alcoholic should have sought pardon and amendment insofar as this is prudent under the particular circumstances. There should at least be openness on his or her part to accomplish this. In the case of children of the marriage, there ought to be the same effort made and parental responsibilities ought to be shared, insofar as this is reasonable and possible. The Twelfth Step should continue these meaningful relationships, if they can be reinstated. What is all important is that the divorced or separated alcoholic does not enclose himself or herself behind a wall of resentments.

In the process of recovery, practicing AA principles in all our affairs at work and in the community is a real challenge. Resentments can easily arise in us in our response to doubts, suspicions, even hatred for us. Some people will not believe in our recovery. They may be important people, who can put us down. They may be "the very good people" in the respectable firm, or neighbors in our community. We come to see the Twelfth Step as a focusing of all the principles of the AA Steps in our lives. At times it means living with difficulties, enduring them not with a stoic grin, but with a joyful serenity in our real recovery. There is much that we can be thankful for in our assets. The AA fellowship, representative as it is in all walks of life, contributes greatly to the acceptance of the social role of the recovering alcoholic. We are really not a people put down, unless we want to indulge in self-pity.

For many reasons, which have nothing to do with alcoholism, we can have grim days and bad times. It is a part of the game of life. It is not without reason that AA people show remarkable qualities of endurance in the hard times. Our practice of AA principles in all our affairs equips us with moral reinforcements. This is already well known in the workaday world to the advantage of the recovering alcoholic. Special assets of personal honesty, courage, loyalty, and fortitude are personality traits in maturity in the Twelfth Step. These social virtues are sought after in the business world and the community at large. Humility in recovery dynamics does not suppress initiative and competition in our affairs; rather it cultivates these drives in building human endeavor in us.

The Twelfth Step, however, is no guarantee to transform the recovering alcoholic into a superstar, to bring success in business or community status. For many of us it means living our ordinary role of life well in normal living. For some of us our alcoholism was symptomatic of intemperance in striving for the exceptional, reaching beyond the horizons of our personal capacities and circumstances. Practicing the AA principles in all our affairs for all of us means a temperance in our strivings, so that the American dream of the good life does not become a nightmare.

Freely We Received. Freely We Give to Others in Need

As we practice AA principles in all our affairs, we cannot neglect to give to other fellow alcoholics what we have freely received from other AA members in our fellowship. Some feel that they satisfy this commitment by attending meetings, telling their stories of failures and successes, keeping the fellowship going. They forget their own hard beginnings in AA. Rare is the man or woman who came to AA on his or her own will power. We came because some other AA person was interested in giving us what was freely given to him. Our staying with the program was due to his or her repeated efforts, even seeking us out again when we faltered. There were times when they were our strength, as we came out of an alcoholic bout, weak and afraid.

Now that we have matured in our recovery, can we forget others in similar need, in real need of understanding support? Have we become too respectable to help drunks? Do we fail to understand alcoholic frailty because we are now so strong? We need not search for these people in lounges and bars. They are at AA meetings. We could be the sponsor they need. We could be the person who could get to them over coffee after the meeting. For the most part, AA people generously respond to this concern and commitment. We consider it a privilege to pass on the way of recovery that is for us the joy of living. Perhaps the greatest reward in helping another is that we are helping ourselves. We are building the human more solidly in our lives. And as always, we receive more from the program than we give.

Twelfth Step work in aiding fellow alcoholics is an art that AA people, faithful to and seasoned in the Steps, are equipped for by living the program. The one practicing the Twelfth Step is not acting as a physician to medicate the sick, or a psychiatrist to analyze alcoholic behavior. The one practicing the Twelfth Step is an understanding friend, sharing and caring, practically knowledgeable in the art of struggling out of the obsession and addiction of alcoholism.

Out of life-experience of the fears, insecurities, doubts and misunderstandings of the beginner's First Step of admission, the chaos of the alcoholic's home, the unmanageability of life, we share generously with those in need of our help. But more than all this misfortune, there is the positive experience of hope, strength, courage, belief in, and surrender to the Higher Power that we pass on. In this way the power of recovery passes from one person to another. The weak are vitally charged by the strong in the fellowship in the dynamics of this God-centered program. It is in truth a reality therapy.

Some of us are more gifted than others in Twelfth Step work. It is difficult to give a formula for this success. In some it is a gift of good humor that excites human interest, an easy manner of approach, a faculty to communicate reasonably and emotionally genuine self-confidence, sincerity and courage of endurance when the person being helped appears unbelieving and falters. Those practicing the Twelfth Step themselves have to be prepared for failures in helping others. When the person helped returns to drinking, it is paramount that those practicing the Twelfth Step visit him or her with another matured AA member. It is safer not to go it alone, not only to assure more help for another, but to ensure our own continued sobriety.

The Not-So-Good Samaritan

There is the real danger that we become too possessive of people whom we help, that we consider the new member a product of our sobriety and forget that this is a God-given gift. There is need for prudence and temperance in success and failure in Twelfth Step work. After experiencing initial help, fellow recovering alcoholics gradually come to look to our direction. We fall into the role of sponsor in the course of time. At this point, however, new members can become overly dependent on us; we must see that they cultivate personal decision as a sign of their recovery. Beginners are especially in danger of scruples in receiving our help. They can give in to being too passive, too suspicious of themselves. Women in the first stages of the recovery process are particularly open to this pitfall. For obvious reasons, it is generally better that a married man does not sponsor a recovering woman alcoholic. There are circumstances, of course, where this would not be true. It is a matter of prudent judgment. We must watch out for the game of the not-so-good Samaritan that can be played in many subtle guises.

Those practicing the Twelfth Step sometimes enjoy a record of successes with recovering fellow alcoholics. They may come to be regarded as champions of total abstinence and a sobriety of moral quality. They may have gained many years of honest and humble living in the AA way of life. Yet even in their ranks there can be falls, as the record shows. No one of us is ever cured, thoroughly sanitized from the recurrence of active alcoholism. We are sometimes amazed to hear a veteran member, a man supposedly of all seasons of sobriety, admit fear of a fall in a new season of perhaps vague discontent. It reminds us of the mistaken notion of success in recovery — the success that has conquered "all problems." The Twelfth Step was never meant to mean this, to be taken as a final step in a finished program. No recovering alcoholic is perfect. Is anybody perfect? How strange that we sometimes expect a recovering alcoholic to be perfect in recovery, somehow never to have shaky times! Obviously such perfect recovery is not to be found in other diseases. And this disease is for life. There is practical wisdom in the AA caution for all the Steps: Easy does it for each twenty-four hours.

Recovery Joys

It is part of the moral miracle of AA that notwithstanding the risk, the gamble of life, members grow in comfortable sobriety that brings the joy of living into personal existence. This serenity is especially a Twelfth Step blessing. Call it the joy of spiritual awakening, the joy of living the program in all one's affairs, the joy of helping fellow alcoholics in need. This is no self-hypnosis, no narcissism, no ego-trip in self-complacency. Rather it is the humble and honest satisfaction of recovering the human, the human that is made in the image of a loving God.

There are some critics of AA, who in their emphasis on the rational in recovery, in objectively ferreting out the causes of alcoholic illness, somehow miss the life-value of human emotions. For them "emotional" is not a scientific word in recovery. Emotionalism has come to mean an unbalanced sentimental state in which the rational is put down. Joy as an emotional condition is not a key word in their recovery programming. Fortunately the mental health field is becoming more humanly oriented. After all, these disciplines are not studying phenomena like the science of physics. They are studying the human, and the human is really both emotional and rational. A person is more than a mind.

Dr. Harry M. Tiebout, the first eminent psychiatrist to take an interest in AA work, observed how AA changes emotions by using emotions. Emotions can be used for good or bad. Tiebout observed how the zest for the joy in drinking is changed into the joys of integral living by the AA way of life. He understood how AA people put their lives together from a divided, fragmented self into an integrated self through an emotional purgation. Meaningful joy is the test of authentic living. A thoroughly rationalized sobriety can produce a well programmed person, but not a vitally recovering person. A person is more than mind, and life is more than the life of reason. Life is the whole man, body and spirit, sense, reason, and will in living with others. Emotion in the proper sense is the expression of the whole man, sensing, reasoning, willing in the total experience of the true, the good, and the beautiful, as well as the false, the bad, and the ugly. The joy of living comes in the total engagement of the whole person. Tiebout saw all this in the AA way of life. It is the discovery of a magnificent possession in recovery, the discovery of the God-given life, a life released from alcoholic obsession.

Understanding Recovery

Recovery must come to be understood in these life terms. It is far more than an algebra of abstracts, more than a pill taking time-table, more than withdrawal from a drug. It is just being human again, as God intended us to be. In our vocabulary the main life-recovery words are not science or technique. They are the personal God and the human person. We must be prepared for great misunderstanding in this, as if we are speaking an alien language to people who see recovery only in pills, chemistry, and technical devices. We must realize the unique experience that comes to us in personal recovery. We have come a long way in knowing what is wrong with us, not just as alcoholics, but as persons, and we are learning what to do about it. The world around us for many people is a world enveloped in the gathering gloom of pessimism, scepticism, and the vital shock of the devaluing of all of life's values.

We live in a period of severe cultural revolution that involves poignantly the young in the struggle to be. We are seeing more and more of the young come to AA in search for understanding of their dependency problem, in the abuse of ethyl alcohol and other drugs. This is a new breed of addicted alcoholics, who speak in a different idiom and seem to hit bottom fast. Many of them want to turn on in the really good life, rather than to cop out. AA people have a special message for them, because we are the real cop-outs who made it back to where the action really is.

To come full cycle from Step One to Step Twelve is not just to have made the program to complete recovery. Rather it is an introduction to life-recovery that must be renewed, gone over, and continued in the changes of life, in the realism that life is change, and that we are never ex-alcoholics, cured people. There is always the life-style of arresting the disease, living with it, knowing our liabilities and our assets. It is by no means the saga of a physical tragedy. The human body has incredible resistance to breakdown when enlivened by a sound spirit. As we grow in AA as persons, our lives open more and more to the joy of living and the serenity of achievement. But this can never mean the joy of complacency, a Disneyland sort of merriment, nor can serenity mean the serenity of rest, as if we have it made. Life is ever unfinished. Each day is a new day, the first day of the rest of our lives. We are ever engaged in building the human in us, rekindling the Divine spark of life in us. *This is what understanding the recovering alcoholic is all about.*

The theme of this book is not mainly alcoholism. It is the person in the life-endeavor to recover from alcoholism, symptomatic of other defects. Alcoholism is a most abstruse subject that easily divides the experts when they attempt to formulate the exact nature of the disease. Although it ranks among the top destroyers of human life, it is not receiving the all-out scientific research and public concern merited by other diseases such as cancer or heart disease. We are popularly more uptight about smoking than we are of our drinking problems. Really it is a moral miracle that AA is able to achieve the success that it has amidst this groundswell of indifference. It is unique that among all the diseases, AA should emerge not as an outgrowth of professional research or popular concern, but as a Twelfth Step of two recovering alcoholics who had experienced a spiritual awakening and began to practice it in all their affairs, and especially to relate it to the needs of other fellow alcoholics. In those days of difficult beginnings in the Thirties, experts in evaluating AA chances for succeeding would have predicted nothing but failure. What resulted is a moral miracle, incredible, but true.

XIII. Live and Let Live

God grant me the Serenity
To accept the things I cannot change
The Courage to change the things I can
And the Wisdom to know the difference.
  The Serenity Prayer

Understanding the Recovering Alcoholic is written in the spirit of understanding recovery in the AA experience. It is a perspective of life-recovery from inside alcoholism in the tradition of AA anonymity. The aim of this book is to essay an understanding of recovery for the alcoholic in search of personal recovery and for those significant others — spouse, parents, friends, employers, clergy, anyone concerned in need of understanding what recovery means for the alcoholic in the AA fellowship.

There is a real need in the professional fields for understanding the living art of the alcoholic's recovery from people experiencing the process. There is a model here worthy of serious insight which carries over into the total drug scene in which alcohol dependence plays a central role along with other drugs. AA today is aiding many polydrug dependents in their route to recovery. Furthermore, there is something for everyone to learn in these reflections about the art of celebrating life amidst a rapidly sickening society.

Life, to be worth living, involves the need of pathways to recovery. In our artificial world, we are all so very open to losing something of our humanity. All of us are in need of recovering something of the healthy human in us. In the great speed of today's living we rush along so very fast that we seem to outrun our very natures. We become like tumble weeds, hollow inside, ever turning and increasing in appearances, yet internally a great ball of emptiness in the wind. How well the recovering alcoholic knows this image. It is in the quiet times that the human in us can come alive, and really look at life. What is it all about? Too many of us get so caught up in the "what" that we never reach the "it." Perhaps it is better that way, because we would discover how we reduced ourselves to an "it," maybe a big "it," but really just an "it."

Life is never an "it," an object. Life is "I," a person with other persons in the creation-continuing process of the God of love. It is time that we learn to put down the oversell of our *objective* questions and come to the personal questions in the art of living. What am I all about? I was all about alcohol, the world of things. Life is living the human, the divinely human. AA has awakened us to this way of seeing, of valuing.

To experience personal relaxation, the serenity of being human is really a turning on to life. It is to learn to relax with oneself, to be able to be in harmony with one's own spirit. This is an art of personal living, of being alive in one's own existence, the hero of one's own life, free from the poisons of resentment and arrogance. It is a far, far journey from the old days of relaxing with a glass crutch, numbing one's consciousness with the sedations of ethyl alcohol because we could not face the truth about ourselves. We were not relaxed with ourselves. To be with oneself was to be with a headache, and so we tranquilized ourselves. We feared being alone without a glass. It was like being without our identity, like being naked in a crowd.

This was no easy matter turning away from the old habits of false relaxation. Going to a party was like going into combat, to search and destroy the easy "yes" to a drink, the drive to join in drinking with the crowd. Did we ever drink *with* a crowd? Maturing in AA is always learning to relax with oneself and through oneself with others. When the challenge is offered us: "What will you have to drink?" we now realize that *we do not just drink. Alcoholics do not just drink. They addict themselves.* The human role for us is to abstain to live, each in his or her own style of positive living. After all, there is more to a party than the contents of a glass, and if that is all the party is, we should not be there.

The art of relaxation is indeed a most important element in recovery. All of our alcoholic stories began with the search for

142

some kind of relief, a bad ego-trip that recovered into a good ego-trip of really discovering ourselves in the AA style of living. *Yes, there is such a thing as a good ego-trip, a finding of true self-love and self-esteem. Genuine recovery demands that it be so. "Love your neighbor as yourself" is the key to real living.*

The recovery, hopefully, is life-long. It is all very common-place, as common as the human in us, and the grounding of the human in the Divine, open to all of us. What is important is not the person telling the story, but the vital principles that weave a pattern of recovery open to fellow humans in need. In our life-style in our community, the sober majority would never discover us. We are anonymous. Live and let live!

The art of the serene sober life is a gift that belongs to the art of living. This is the ideal of the recovering alcoholic. Science concerns principles of control and prediction of phenomena. Art is a way of producing, in this case the practical art of living for the recovering alcoholic. Presently some alcohologists are questioning the disease concept of alcoholism and the criterion of total sobriety as the success-measure of treatment. There is even experimentation in controlled drinking as "a cure for alcoholism." The debate goes on in the complex world of theories. The alcoholic who wants recovery in the meantime must have his or her recovery route, or be destroyed, not as an idea in a debate, but as a person in life. Alcoholics have accomplished this recovery route by founding the fellowship of Alcoholics Anonymous.